The Write Stuff

The Write Stuff

Crafting Sermons That Capture and Convince

Sondra B. Willobee

Book design by Sharon Adams
Cover design by Jennifer K. Cox

First edition
Published by Westminster John Knox Press
Louisville, Kentucky

This book is printed on acid-free paper that meets the American National Standards Institute Z39.48 standard. ♾

09 10 11 12 13 14 15 16 17 18 — 10 9 8 7 6 5 4 3 2 1

Library of Congress Cataloging-in-Publication Data

Willobee, Sondra B.
The write stuff : crafting sermons that capture and convince / Sondra B. Willobee. — 1st ed.
p. cm.
ISBN 978-0-664-23281-8 (alk. paper)
1. Preaching. 2. Authorship. I. Title.

BV4211.3.W56 2009
251—dc22

2008022115

For my husband

Contents

Acknowledgments

I am grateful to many people, especially the congregations of Farmington and South Lyon First United Methodist Churches, who taught me more than they know. An enormous thank you goes to Tom Long and Zan Holmes, without whose advocacy this book probably would not have been published. Thank you to my editors at Westminster John Knox Press: Jack Keller, who endured with grace while I stalked him at the Festival of Faith and Writing, and Gavin Stephens, who picked up the project midway with patience and professionalism.

Members of my writers' group—Dick, Bobbie, Norma, Sarah, and John—marked up countless drafts. Mary Jo's wonderful poetry workshops kept my love of words alive even when I was buried under work at the church. Thank you to Ellen Acton, who proofread the entire manuscript, to Laura Willobee, a scrupulous permissions assistant, and to Barbara Willobee, a magician in Paint, who always asked, "Did you work on your book today?"

I've learned so much from students, professors, colleagues, workshop leaders, and writing instructors it's impossible to thank them all. I'll always remember my first class with Dr. Robert Tannehill, however, whose imaginative rendering of the context of the Gospel of Mark made me put down my pen and simply listen.

John Shewell, that blessed curmudgeon, told me I had to write this book. Barbara Lewis-Lakin always believed in me. My husband, Ed, fellow canoeist and companion, has been steady as a heartbeat.

These are some in my great cloud of witnesses. May we who preach run with perseverance the race that is set before us, looking to Jesus the pioneer and perfecter of our faith.

Foreword

Pastors of congregations, many of whom preach forty or more sermons annually, produce the written equivalent of a novel every year. And that doesn't count the endless newsletter articles, funeral reflections, wedding homilies, annual reports, and retreat reflections. Small wonder that pastors sometimes view the ministry's ceaseless demand for fresh material as if it were the cannibalistic plant, "Audrey Junior," in *The Little Shop of Horrors*, singing, "Feed me, feed me, feed me, Seymour!"

Inevitably, given the relentless return of the Sabbath, the wells of creativity are drawn low, and the flow of sparkling sermon ideas is reduced to a trickle. Sermon after sermon seems tired, desiccated, flat. As a preacher myself who has often experienced this loss of imagination, I am comforted by the words of so gifted a writer as Mary Gordon, who said of writers, "Most of us awake paraphrasing words from the *Book of Common Prayer*, horrified by what we have done, what we have left undone, convinced that there is no health in us."

For such seasons of sermonic drought, Sondra B. Willobee's *The Write Stuff* is a refreshing spring rain. She knows that what releases a torrent of inspiration in preaching is often not climbing a high mountain to gain some grand and sweeping vista but instead small things—taking an unusual sight line in a biblical text, raising a provocative question, or turning off the computer and paying attention to what is happening around us. Author William Saroyan notes how much good writing starts with little things. It can begin "by remembering a tree in the backyard," he says, which leads the imagination into the parlor where there is a piano, and on the piano is a photograph of a younger brother who was killed in the war. From the small to the powerfully human.

Willobee is a seasoned pastor and preacher, and she is not hesitant to reach into her memory and experience to share her own successes and failures in the pulpit. She is also not afraid to see the fashioning of good sermons not only as a matter of prayer, inspiration, and openness to the Spirit but also of good old-fashioned trial and error. "Try this," she suggests repeatedly, practically, and helpfully. "And if that doesn't work, then try that." A good sermon is like the Brooklyn Bridge—lovely to behold with its graceful catenary curves and soaring Gothic towers—but it is also the product of sound engineering and trustworthy infrastructure. Willobee grasps both sides of this equation: the artistic splendor of good sermons but also the bricks, mortar, and architectural design that make such beauty possible. Without losing sight of the final goal, that is, testimony worthy to honor God, Willobee takes us to the drafting table to consider how the working pieces of a sermon are crafted and fitted together. Preachers are like all other writers who wish to craft prose into a house of beauty. As Susan Sontag once said, they "work in a lumberyard of words."

This is a fine book for preachers, for those who are just beginning the journey of preaching and for those veterans who are returning to the garage for a 100,000-mile checkup. As Willobee says in this book, "We preachers work attentively within a long tradition, crafting as carefully as we can a thing of beauty, delighting in the play of detail and form." I cannot imagine a more practical, attentive, useful, reliable, provocative, and thoughtful guide to the delightful play of detail and form in sermons than this volume.

Thomas G. Long
Candler School of Theology
Emory University
Atlanta, GA

Introduction

Gravity is having its way with me. Maybe that's why I've been noticing sagging in other places. High school students slouched over desks. Working parents slumped over kitchen tables. The Michigan economy still dragging its feet. As a preacher, however, what especially worries me is sagging sermons.

You know the signs of a sagging sermon. Looking out at the congregation, you see drooping eyes, downcast gazes, listless faces. A woman scribbles a grocery list. The head of the trustees lets loose a yawn. If you scanned the energy level of the congregation, it would read _____. The sermon isn't going anywhere, isn't doing anything. And the only thing worse than listening to a sagging sermon is delivering one.

I remember one of my worst sermons. I was invited to preach during homecoming weekend at my alma mater, a small liberal arts college. The service was held in a cavernous chapel designed for a thousand people. Less than one hundred were scattered through the pews. The largest part of the congregation, the college choir, was seated behind me, many of them pale and puffy-eyed.

Not good.

Though a few listeners chuckled at my opening comments, by the second paragraph, I could feel the congregation slipping away.

Feet shuffled in the choir loft behind me. There were repeated coughs. An elderly woman rummaged in her capacious purse for a mint. My beloved professor, on whose recommendation I'd been invited, put on an expression of patient cheer. When it was all over, I just wanted to slink away.

A colleague told me that most preachers are too overwhelmed week by week to worry about improving their sermons. I don't believe that's true. We want to honor God with our preaching. We want to tell the world in the most powerful way possible the good news of Jesus Christ. Worship is the event with the highest visibility that reaches the largest percentage of our people. Collectively, we preachers hold a great number of persons hostage in boredom or frustration when our sermons sag. "Boredom is a form of evil," Fred Craddock said. "It works against the faith by provoking contrary thoughts or lulling to sleep or draping the whole occasion with a pall of indifference."[1] Sagging sermons suggest that Christianity can safely be ignored.

When we fail to reach people, it is not usually for lack of conviction or effort or sincerity on our part. Rather, as happened for me that homecoming morning, our preaching usually falters for lack of craft. Though the setting contributed to my difficulties that day, my real problem was sermon design. Weak introduction, vague application, and slow narrative pulse. Too often, pressed by the demands of impossible schedules, we shortchange the process of shaping the message so that it can be heard.

Writers Can Help

This is where writers can help us. Good writers know how to grab and hold attention. They can show us how to create a compelling opening ("hook"), how to generate suspense through structure ("book"), and how to arouse interest with vivid language ("stone"). When she was asked where to find good books on preaching, Barbara Brown Taylor sent preachers not to the seminary library but to the creative-writing section of the bookstore. Fred Craddock urged preachers to read good literature in order to enhance their use of language and help them arrange their material for maximum impact.[2] This book condenses material on the creative-writing shelf for busy pastors.

Yes, our sermons must do more than dazzle. A sermon is not made strong by tricks and gimmicks. But our people cannot judge the value of our ideas if they've quit listening. And in these difficult times since 9/11, it's even more important to help our congregations hear the word of God. Anxiety crackles in the air as people lose jobs, and with them, health insurance. Loved ones worry about soldiers deployed in repeated rotations, coming home maimed or not at all. College graduates cannot find work, hard-pressed families are foreclosed from their homes. Our people suffer. So much is at stake. We cannot afford to lose their attention and squander the opportunity to bring them the good news of Jesus Christ.

The Word-Work of God

Lest we panic or despair, it helps to remember that preachers participate in a work that is already underway. It began long before us. The book of Genesis tells us that God brought creation into being by speaking an energetic word. "God said . . . let there be . . . and it was so . . . and God made . . . and God saw that it was good." The refrain that threads its way through Genesis 1 shows how creation began in speech and ended in delight. Terence Fretheim suggested that the phrase "let there be" invites created things to participate in the ongoing work of creation. "The receptor of the word helps shape the result," Fretheim said.[3]

Sometimes, however, God must break apart a world to create something new. God spoke through the prophets to challenge idolatry and oppression so that a new order of love and justice might prevail. The "word of the Lord," *ha-dabar Elohim*, exposed corruption, dethroned rulers, comforted exiles, and envisioned a new creation. Jesus, the Logos, Word-made-flesh, was the ultimate expression of God's creative and redemptive speech. His words, indeed, his very self, brought near to his hearers the kingdom of God.

It seems presumptuous to think that we preachers participate in the word-work of God, this work begun at creation, continued in the prophets, and culminated in Christ. And yet we do. Because Jesus expected it. "Greater works than these," he said (John 14:12). Through the power of the Holy Spirit, our sermons join in God's work to shape and transform the world.

"But I'm not very creative," some might say. Pish. Creativity is part of the nature given us by God. Songwriter Michael Card put it this way: "Anyone who says they are not creative really means they do not measure up to other well-known people who in general make their living from writing or painting or such. . . . You deny your true nature when you exclude yourself from the creative process, as one who was created by a God who calls us to reflect his image in the world."[4]

How to Use This Book

This book includes exercises that are designed to help writers tap their latent creative powers. Tagged by the heading "Try This," such exercises include directed meditation, free-writing, clustering, sensory exploration, and experimenting with simple forms. Like scales for a musician, these exercises expand our range and purify our tone. Or, like a fitness regimen, they increase our flexibility and strength as we heft ideas and press their weight.

Imaginative exercises used by writers can also help us outwit what I call "the Censor" and "the Production Manager." The Censor says, "You can't say that. What will people think?" The Censor shuts down exploration before it's even started. The Production Manager says, "Quit messing around. You've got calls to make, people to counsel, and meetings to plan. Come up with something—now!" Pressure from the Production Manager obstructs the flow of fresh ideas. Imagination-stretching exercises provide a way to sidestep these internal critics until we are well underway.

Try This

Sit comfortably in a chair, feet flat, hands cupped open on your knees. Close your eyes and breathe deeply several times. On each inhale, speak or think the words, "Fill me." On each exhale, say the words, "Holy Spirit." Next, read aloud these sentences from Genesis 1:2–3: "The earth was without form, and void; and darkness was upon the face of the deep. And the Spirit of God moved upon the face of the waters" (KJV).

Choose three of the words from those verses. They could be "earth, waters, deep" or "God, void, face" or any combination you choose. Free-write for five minutes about any images or memories you associate with those words. Let the thoughts come out in a jumble. Don't worry about coherence, punctuation, or grammar. Every time you get stuck, write the three words again and keep going. After the five minutes are up, put the writing aside and don't look at it for at least a week. When you go back to it, underline one sentence that seems to have energy or expresses a new thought. If you are a lectionary preacher, look up when Genesis 1 occurs in the lectionary and write a note to yourself to revisit the free-writing exercise then.

Revel in Craft

Some preachers worry that too much attention to technique makes sermons calculated rather than inspired. After all, Matthew 10:19 says, "Do not worry about how you are to speak or what you are to say; for what you are to say will be given to you at that time." To dismiss craft, however, is to refuse the gifts of those who communicated the words of God through the ages. Prophets used imagery, plays on words, parables, and proverbs to get their hearers' attention. Jesus used aphorisms, riddles, and hyperbole, as well as his distinctive parables, to cajole and convict. Paul employed every weapon from the arsenal of rhetoric to quell his critics and strengthen his congregations. Poet John Ciardi told of an incident in which one of Robert Frost's hearers was offended by Frost's description of the "technical tricks" in his poems such as rhyme, repetition, and metaphor. "Surely when you are writing one of your bee-oo-ti-ful poems," Frost's critic said, "surely you are not thinking of technical tricks!" Frost thought for a second or two, then leaned into the microphone to reply in a playful tone, "I revel in 'em."[5] Technique, in fact, was how Frost achieved his memorable effects. His lovely poem "Stopping by Woods on a Snowy Evening," so seemingly simple and graceful, has a complex quadruple rhyme scheme and ends with a powerful repetition of the penultimate line. Though writing craft is no substitute for exegetical study or theological wrestling, craft helps us to communicate what we have heard and known. As Eugene Lowry said, "All matters of technique have to do, not with the desire to be clever, but rather with the intention to be alive and open to the surprise of the gospel. . . . Sermon preparation is not simply the occasion for our 'creative work,' but for the work of God."[6]

Hard Work

Good preaching, then, is hard work. In preaching we try to be faithful to God, the Scriptures, the congregation, and ourselves—all at the same time. We're also held accountable by the communion of the saints. We remember prophets who risked the wrath of kings to proclaim a word from the Lord. We follow apostles who gave up homes and families and livelihoods to witness to Jesus. We're indebted to martyrs whose shed blood proclaimed the gospel. We have our own personal "cloud of witnesses" as well, mentors living and dead, those pastors, teachers, parents, grandparents, spouses, children, and friends who sit invisibly watching us as we write and speak. The scholarly community also weighs in. From office shelves lined with glossy volumes of *The New Interpreter's Bible* and multicolored dust jackets of Westminster's Old Testament Library, the scholars whisper, "What is the history of interpretation of this passage? Have you expressed the heart of the Scripture?" Faced with all this, I want to go to the refrigerator, squeeze chocolate syrup into a tablespoon, and take it straight.

When we step into the pulpit, we also bear the weight of congregational need. A secretary with thoracic cancer. A computer programmer out of work for two years. A mother struggling with alcoholism. A family devastated by suicide. We wrestle with the questions people have brought to us. Why did this happen to me, Pastor? Why doesn't God answer my prayers? If not dealing with crises, our people are just trying to muster the daily persistence to make it through the week. Often we are doing that, too.

Yet we are still committed to excellence. In the movie *Chariots of Fire*, two chancellors at Oxford University criticized Olympic hopeful Harold Abrams because he employed a personal trainer to prepare for the one-hundred-meter dash. They preferred "the way of the amateur." Abrams retorted, "You want victory as much as I do, but with the apparent effortlessness of gods."[7] We are not amateurs, we are not gods, but we want the victory of the gospel. So, like the Olympic runner who lifts weights, logs laps, and submits to a trainer's critique, we practice the disciplines of our craft. We pray. We study. We listen. We write. We revise. We practice, and revise again. Then, feeling ready or not, we lay ourselves open to the moment when our words fall into the air between pulpit and pew, when our offering becomes that mysterious creation of the Holy Spirit and the whole community of faith.

Indeed, the Holy Spirit is at work throughout the process of preaching, from the private hours in our study to the public proclamation from the pulpit. When I have been sweating over the shape of a sermon, get up to do something else, and the perfect transition plops itself into my mind, that's the Holy Spirit. When a parishioner's face lights up with new insight, or relaxes into an acceptance of God's love, that's the Holy Spirit, too, and the hairs on my arms stand up. When a sermon works, when we can see in our hearers' eyes and faces that they are listening, when the sermon moves them to deeper faith or decisive commitment, and when, by the power at work in us, the sermon accomplishes abundantly far more than all we could ask or imagine, it is pure joy.

Hook

Chapter One

Use a Hook

Which sermon is more likely to catch your parishioners' attention? One that begins, "Today I'm going to talk about Paul's doctrine of election," or one that begins, "Her sister stood, as she always did, smack in the middle of the doorway with her arms folded and her right hip cocked. She was grinning a smug little grin. Though the door was open, there was no way Celeste could get through. She figured it would be like that in heaven, too."

We know that how we begin a sermon is important. If we don't capture our hearers right away, they may drift off to daydream or doodle on the bulletin. Wary, distracted, sophisticated, or jaded, our listeners are harder than ever to reach. Preachers are affected by the same erosion of authority that has undercut all leaders since the sixties. I was teaching a Sunday morning Bible study on the passage in which Jesus says, "It is easier for a camel to go through the eye of a needle than for someone who is rich to enter the kingdom of God" (Mark 10:17–27). The class talked about what this Scripture meant for us as Christians in the United States. One participant, a lawyer who owned two homes and several cars, kept trying to find loopholes. Finally I said, "Though Jesus uses exaggerated language here, his teachings on riches add up to the same thing: wealth puts our souls in peril." The lawyer looked straight at me and said, "Well, that's just your opinion."

Even if our parishioners grant us authority to preach, it's hard to keep their attention. They are bombarded by sound bites, overstimulated by entertainment, and overwhelmed by the demands of family, household, and career. The rapid pace of television and video games has trained them to be impatient. (My daughters are always telling me to talk faster when I preach.) The sophistication of our media culture has also raised expectations for quality of presentation. In my lifetime we've moved from chalkboard to whiteboard to overhead projector to PowerPoint, which is now being done by second-graders. We compete with advertising agencies that spend millions of dollars to hire the most creative minds in the nation. After Super Bowl Sunday, our parishioners are more likely to remember what the lizard said about the ferret than what Jesus said about the Pharisees.[1]

Accustomed to the seduction of advertising, our hearers may come to church expecting to be manipulated. They are rightly suspicious if it seems we, too, are trying to sell them something. As Paul told the Corinthians, "We are not peddlers of God's word" (2 Cor. 2:17). However, our hearers may also be sitting in the pews with their arms crossed and their jaws set because they know God intends to mess in their business. I've sat in worship services looking narrowly at the preacher for just that reason. I remember one Sunday in particular, after a fight with my husband. I knew I would probably hear something in my colleague's sermon that would challenge the ugly words I had flung the night before. I did. It was good for me, but it was hard to listen. The resistance of our parishioners may extend to skipping church altogether. Fred Craddock told his students to assume their listeners almost didn't come to church that morning.[2]

Despite their resistance, our people are hungry for meaning. We want to capture and keep their attention long enough for them to hear a word that gives life. For journalists and writers, the opening of an article, essay, or story is called the "hook." A hook dangles something that is important to the listener. A hook incites interest, establishes the speaker's credibility, sets the tone, and suggests something about the theme. Hooks also tell our hearers how to listen to the rest of what we are going to say, just as "Once upon a time . . ."

prepares us for a fairy tale or "A man walked into a bar . . ." signals a joke. The hook Jesus used in Luke 15:11, "There was a man who had two sons," invited his audience into an intimate story of family relationships. The stylized language and elevated tone, however, suggested that the story was going to be about much more than this one family. His hearers expected Jesus to say something important about their own relationships and about God.

Start a Fight

Conflict is a great hook. An old Irish proverb said, "If you want someone's attention, start a fight." Author Barnaby Conrad discussed why conflict is a good hook in his book *The Complete Guide to Writing Fiction:*

> Which story, for example, would you be most interested in reading? One that began like this: "Their annual picnic was always a peaceful, joyous outing where everyone got along" or "Usually, their annual picnic had been a peaceful, joyous outing where everyone got along. And, at first, that's the way it was this July 4, 1990."
>
> Implicit in the second example is that the picnic we are reading about was not so peaceful, not so joyous, and everyone didn't get along. Why? We want to read further to find out what went wrong, what the trouble was, what happened. Trouble! . . .
>
> We don't like trouble in real life, we don't like problems, we don't like conflict, yet we love to *read* about how people cope with trouble: marital trouble, martial trouble, parental trouble, trouble with cops, trouble with crops, people with addictions, people with afflictions.[3]

As writing teacher Janet Burroway explained, "In literature, *only* conflict is interesting. This is not so in life. Life offers periods of comfortable communication, peaceful pleasure, and productive work, all of which are extremely interesting to those involved. But passages about such times make for dull reading."[4] And dull preaching.

The Bible pulses with conflict. In scene after scene, characters push and pull against each other, powerful forces are invoked and opposed. In Exodus, for example, Moses and Pharaoh engaged in an epic contest of wills. In the Gospels, Jesus castigated the Pharisees; they, in turn, plotted to kill him. Jesus battled the demons that silence, sicken, and convulse human beings. The disciples competed with each other for prominence. In the sixth chapter of Acts, Greek-speaking Christians complained that their widows were being neglected in the food distribution. In his letters, Paul lambasted the "super-apostles" who discredited his ministry.

Tension may also exist within the Scripture between an earlier version of the text and later editors who shaped the materials for the needs of their communities. The Deuteronomistic editor of the Pentateuch, for example, repressed the loose loyalties of the old tribal confederacy in favor of centralizing power in Jerusalem. Mark shaped his explanation of the parable of the sower to highlight the dangers of apostasy because his hearers were falling away under persecution.

We can also feel the friction in the Scriptures between faith communities and other powers in the world. Mark's community, for example, struggled against persecution from Roman rulers. John's people lashed out at the religious leaders, family, and former friends who cast them out of the synagogue. The Christian community at Corinth had to assert itself against the lures of paganism and dissolute living. And the author of 1 Peter warned that "like a roaring lion your adversary the devil prowls around, looking for someone to devour" (5:8).

Or the trouble may be lodged within human nature itself. When Paul said, "For I do not do the good I want, but the evil I do not want is what I do" (Rom. 7:19), the tension is between who Paul is and who he wants to be, between the power of sin and the grace of God.

Eugene Lowry suggested that we "look for trouble" when we begin our exegesis. "What is there about the text that does not seem to fit? Is there anything strange here? What is at stake?"[5] He advised preachers to look for the "itch" the Scripture wants to "scratch."[6] "If the narrative process is to be followed," he said, "the sermon will begin—one way or another—with a discrepancy, a conflict, an ambiguity needing resolution."[7]

Barbara Brown Taylor began her sermon on Luke 13:1–9, "Life Giving Fear," with a trouble hook:

> When I was a hospital chaplain, the calls I dreaded most did not come from the emergency room, the psychiatric ward, or even the morgue. They came from the pediatric floor, where little babies lay in cribs with bandages covering half their heads and sweet-faced children pushed IV poles down the hall. One day I received a call to come sit with a mother while her five-year-old daughter was in surgery. Earlier in the week, the girl had been playing with a friend when her head began to hurt. By the time she found her mother, she could no longer see. At the hospital, a CAT scan confirmed that a large tumor was pressing on the girl's optic nerve and she was scheduled for surgery as soon as possible.[8]

Once we hear this opening paragraph, we care about the child, the mother, and the chaplain. Will the little girl make it? How will the mother cope? What will the chaplain say? All of these questions make us want to keep listening. Taylor's hook then set up the issue Jesus voiced in Luke 13:2, "Do you think that because these Galileans suffered in this way they were worse sinners than all other Galileans?" and she was well-launched into her theme of why bad things happen to good people.

Try This

Read Mark 3:19b–30 or 2 Corinthians 12:11–19. What are the conflicts or tensions within the text, stated or implied? What entities are opposed to each other? What is at stake for each of them? Write a hook that sets out the conflict.

Set a Big Hook

Conflict may be sketched very broadly. In his novel *A Tale of Two Cities*, Charles Dickens opened with a hook of large-scale conflict:

"It was the best of times; it was the worst of times; it was the age of wisdom; it was the age of foolishness; it was the epoch of belief; it was the epoch of incredulity; it was the season of light; it was the season of darkness; it was the spring of hope; it was the winter of despair; we had everything before us; we had nothing before us; we were all going direct to heaven; we were all going direct the other way."[9] In a similar vein, Frederick Buechner began his sermon on Mark 9:14–31 with a large-scale conflict:

> In this passage from Mark there are really two texts . . . [that] stand in the most violent sort of contrast with one another, a contrast that seems ironic even to the point of blasphemy. And the realities to which the two texts point are equally at odds, and the contrast between them is just as violent and ironic. Because the first text deals with the power of God and the second one deals with the power of man, and the printed page is almost torn in two by having to bear them both, just as this world is almost torn in two, just as you and I as individuals are almost torn in two, by having to contain them both. This is the great power struggle of our age and of all ages—not East against West, Communism against Democracy, White against Black, but this struggle: man's power against God's power, man against God and God against man.[10]

The large-scale hook is the equivalent of the "long shot" in a movie, the opening scene in a Western, for example, where we see riders on horseback coming over a rise against a backdrop of mountains. The sweep of the landscape establishes that this will be an epic story about the mighty clash of good and evil. A large-scale hook is especially appropriate when preaching thematically on such topics as sin, salvation, theodicy, or eschatology.

Jump in the Middle

"They threw me off the hay truck about noon."[11] This opening sentence in James Cain's novel *The Postman Always Rings Twice* illustrates another kind of hook, what the ancient Roman poet Horace called *in medias res*, "into the middle of things." This hook jumps right into the action. Susan Howatch began *in medias res* in her novel *Mystical Paths:* "I had just returned from an exorcism and was flinging some shirts into the washing machine when my colleague entered the kitchen. He was wearing his cassock and carrying a bottle of whiskey."[12] That opening gets your attention! A sermon I preached on Genesis 32 began *in medias res*:

> Jacob is up against it. His twin brother, Esau, waits for him at the border with an armed company of four hundred men. It is payback for when Jacob cheated Esau of his birthright twenty years ago. Jacob prays a desperate prayer: "God, deliver me from the hand of my brother." Then he comes up with this plan. He divides his company into two groups—oxen, donkeys, sheep and slaves—thinking, "If Esau comes to one company and destroys it, then the company that is left will escape." Jacob also sends ahead a present for his brother, 220 goats, 220 sheep, 30 camels, 50 cows and 20 donkeys. But Jacob himself stays at the very back with his wives and children. Will Esau plunder his possessions and kill Jacob and his family? Only morning will tell.[13]

In medias res works well when you choose to open your sermon with a scene from a real-life incident or from a movie. I used the opening scene from the 1983 movie *Tender Mercies* to begin a sermon on the transforming power of baptism. The main character, Mac Sledge, once a successful songwriter, had deteriorated to being an alcoholic drifter. Over the course of the movie, he put his life back together with the help of a devout Vietnam war widow. When I preached the sermon in 1987, I started out by saying, "I saw a great movie . . ." If I were to preach the sermon again, however, I would *not* begin by recommending the movie, even though it was excellent. I wouldn't even tell the congregation I was talking about a movie. Instead, I would simply describe Mac Sledge facing the proprietor of the motel where his drinking buddy left him:

> A man stands outside the office of a clapboard motel in the flatlands of central Texas. The harsh light of late morning shows all the lines in his face. "How far to the nearest town?" he asks the owner of the motel, a woman in her late twenties.
>
> "Four miles," the woman answers.
>
> "Fella I was with pay for the room, Lady?"
>
> "No."
>
> The man goes back to the motel room, picks up his coat from the rumpled bed, and looks for his wallet. When he doesn't find it, he takes a swig from the whiskey bottle under the coat. He goes back to the office.
>
> "Lady, I'm broke. I'd be glad to work out what I owe you."
>
> "All right," she says carefully. "But there's no drinking while you're working here."
>
> "Yes, ma'am."[14]

After describing the scene, I said, "And this is the beginning of how Mac Sledge was changed." This opener set the stage for a discussion of how baptism works in our lives, changing us before we are even aware of it. Once the hearers are hooked, we can fill in background information as needed and make the transition to the rest of the sermon.

The *in medias res* hook communicates the urgency of the gospel message. The Gospel writer Mark would have loved this kind of hook. Mark repeated the word "immediately" seventeen times in his Gospel, showing Jesus as a decisive man of action. *In medias res* also demonstrates that God regularly breaks into human routines with an offer of grace.

Disclose and Withhold

A hook can incite interest by giving and withholding information at the same time. The opening of Charles Dickens's *A Christmas Carol* does this: "Marley was dead, to begin with."[15] This six-word sentence suggests all kinds of interesting questions: Who is Marley? How did he die? Why does it matter? How is his death a beginning? We will know by the end of the story that his death really was a beginning for Ebenezer Scrooge. Thomas Troeger used a disclosing/withholding hook in his sermon on 1 Corinthians 13:

> It was not your typical hunting accident. It did not involve one man shooting another when he fired blindly into the woods, nor was it a rifle that went off unexpectedly because the safety was not on.
>
> Yes, there were some similarities to the accidents you read about in the papers; it was during deer season and it involved two hunters coming from opposite directions, both stalking the same animal.
>
> But they never fired a shot, although they killed a deer and a bystander.
>
> I don't want to give you all the details right away. If I do, you will remember only the circumstances of Aud's death and never understand my loss.[16]

Troeger's sermon about how we know the love of God through those who love us in this life came to its conclusion during the pastoral prayer following the sermon. With its intimations of violence, love, and death, this hook immediately draws us in.

The disclosing/witholding hook honors the mystery of human life. It suggests that things are not always what they seem. The Gospel writer John may have appreciated this kind of hook. His Gospel slowly reveals who Jesus is by a series of enigmatic signs and multilayered dialogues. This hook would be especially appropriate for a complex sermon that moves inductively, gathering meaning with the introduction of each new idea.

Ask a Question

Posing a question is a time-honored sermonic hook. Question hooks are rarer in fiction than in sermons, but Edgar Allan Poe used a question hook to great effect in his short story "The Tell-Tale Heart." Poe opened the story with this sentence: "True!–nervous–very, very dreadfully nervous I had been and am;

but why will you say that I am mad?"[17] In one artful sentence Poe set the tone, revealed the character of his narrator, and posed the question to haunt the reader—is this narrator trustworthy or not? Likewise, our hooks convey our feelings about our subject and alert our hearers to what comes next.

Jung Young Lee used the question hook in his opening to a sermon on Matthew 10:34–39, first preached with no notes to twelve people in a small North Dakota church:

> This is the most difficult teaching of Jesus that I have ever confronted in my study of the New Testament. Why did Jesus say that he came to bring a sword rather than peace? Do we not call him the Prince of Peace? Did he not say that the peacemakers receive God's blessings? Did he not say that we must go to our brothers for reconciliation before we ask God's forgiveness? How could he then say that he came to destroy the peace and disrupt our family life? Why did he want to break up our family? Is not the family a divine institution? There are countless questions that the text presents to us.[18]

Notice how Lee alluded to a variety of Scripture passages and church teachings, thus increasing the weight of his questions. Benjamin E. Mays employed a question hook in his sermon "Thanksgiving," on Matthew 25:31–46: "This is the Thanksgiving season, and we are justified in raising the following question with hope, faith, skepticism, and pessimism, 'What have we to be thankful for?'"[19] Mays saved his question from being trite and sentimental by naming a sequence of contradictory feelings and ending with the strongest negative one (pessimism). The conflict between the expected seasonal virtue of gratitude and the named feelings creates an interesting tension. We want to know how Mays will resolve it. Questions work as a hook if they are substantive, if they speak to things your listeners care about.

Jesus was a master of questions that "hooked" his hearers: Who do you say that I am? Why did you doubt? Which one was the neighbor? Such questions lodge in the consciousness and work on their hearers long after they are spoken. Because they reveal motives, expand understanding, and pose new possibilities, questions are one of the most popular and useful sermon hooks.

Sketch a Character

You can also begin your sermon by describing a vivid character, such as F. Scott Fitzgerald did early in *The Great Gatsby:* "If personality is a series of successful gestures, then there was something gorgeous about him, some heightened sensitivity to the promises of life, as if he were related to one of those intricate machines that register earthquakes ten thousand miles away."[20] The words *gorgeous, heightened,* and *intricate* suggest that however the narrator feels about him, this Gatsby is a memorable character! Barbara Brown Taylor began with a sketch of a vivid character in her sermon "Out of the Whirlwind":

> We do not hear much about Job in church and yet he remains one of the most compelling figures in the Hebrew Bible. It is that unjustified suffering of his that does it. You can read about Moses splitting the Red Sea or Deborah routing the Canaanites and never once think about your own life, but once Job climbs on his dung heap and starts cursing the day he was born, it is hard not to empathize. Everyone has been there, at one time or another, or at least knows someone who has.[21]

Character hooks function like photos in a family album. Old photos connect us to our ancestors and kinfolk, prompting stories. "Who is this? Where did they come from? Tell me more, Grandpa." Character hooks help our listeners identify with biblical people and imagine themselves within the sweep of salvation history. The author of Hebrews used a character hook to open his letter: "Long ago God spoke to our ancestors in many and various ways by the prophets, but in these last days he has spoken to us by a Son, whom he appointed heir of all things, through whom he also created the worlds" (Heb. 1:1–2). The author used the technique again in chapter 11 when he introduced a series of characters from the Hebrew Scriptures who *make up* the "cloud of witnesses." With character hooks, the preacher turns the pages of the album and invites the congregation to look on.

Say Something Striking

Start your sermon with a memorable statement or an interesting generality, as Leo Tolstoy did in his novel *Anna Karenina*: "Happy families are all alike; every unhappy family is unhappy in its own way."[22] Barbara Brown Taylor uses this technique often, as in her sermon on Judges 6:11–24: "The only thing most of us know about Gideon is that some friends of his have put Bibles in hotel or motel rooms all over the world."[23] To spark interest in a sermon on peace, for example, you might quote Howard Thurman, "During times of war, hatred becomes quite respectable, even though it has to masquerade often under the guise of patriotism."[24] You might add Oscar Wilde's epithet, "Patriotism is the virtue of the vicious."[25] Collections of memorable sayings on a variety of topics are available in print or on the Internet and are well worth reading. Rehearsing the epigrams of great speakers helps sharpen our own wit—we learn from them how to turn a phrase.

When we use strong statements at the outset of a sermon, we must judge whether our hearers will be so intrigued that they sit up and pay attention or so offended that they stop listening altogether. "Virtue of the vicious" might turn some listeners off. The Thurman/Wilde combination above also raises the issue of the moral authority of quoted sources. For most congregations, respected preacher Howard Thurman will have more credibility than the libertine writer Oscar Wilde. Again, you must know your congregation well enough to gauge if the statement will have the intended effect. With its compressed wisdom and indelible phrasing, the memorable statement hook functions like a proverb or aphorism in Wisdom literature. It would be well-suited as an opener to topical or ethical sermons.

Begin with an Image

A budding almond shoot. A tilted cooking pot. Jeremiah saw a message from God in these images. Jesus told of a woman's lost coins and of a lamp on a stand. God sometimes speaks to us through the landscapes and objects of our lives. We can also begin our sermons with an arresting image, as Edmund Steimle did in his Christmas Eve homily "The Eye of the Storm":

> I think I shall never forget the time when hurricane Hazel, back in the fifties, was sweeping through eastern Pennsylvania and hit Philadelphia, where we were living at the time, head on. Unlike most hurricanes, which lose much of their force when they turn inland, this one hit with all the fury of a hurricane at sea: drenching rains, screaming winds, trees uprooted, branches flying through the air, broken power lines crackling on the pavements. It was frightening. Then suddenly there was a letup, a lull. Shortly all was still. Not a leaf quivered. The sun even broke through briefly. It was the eye of the storm. "All was calm, all was bright." And then all hell broke loose again: branches and trees crashing down, the screaming winds, the torrential rain, the power lines throwing out sparks on the pavement. But that was a breathless moment—when we experienced the eye of the storm.
>
> Christmas Eve is something like that, like the experience of the eye of the storm.[26]

A hook like this one accomplishes its effect by engaging as many senses as possible—sight, sound, taste, touch, smell. Steimle did this in one sentence: "drenching rain, screaming winds, trees uprooted, branches flying through the air, broken power lines crackling on the pavements." A preacher, however, cannot linger in description as long as a novelist does—there is just not enough time. I recommend including only those details that catch the hearers, set the tone, and suggest the theme.

What about Jokes?

Many preachers use jokes or funny stories to begin their sermons. Humor loosens up our listeners and creates a warm and lively atmosphere. Jokes work best, however, when they are tightly related to the main theme of the sermon. If it's obvious that you've told a joke just to tell a joke, you haven't started the sermon at all, you've just delayed it by the length of the joke. I used this series of jokes on gender conflict to lead into a sermon on Galatians 3:23–29 about Christian unity :

> Perhaps you've seen some of the e-mails that trade jokes and jabs between men and women. Like these from the women: "Q: How many men does it take to change a roll of toilet paper? A: We don't know; it has never happened." Or, "Q: What is the difference between men and government bonds? A: The bonds mature." And, "Q: Why are married women heavier than single women? A: Single women come home, see what's in the fridge and go to bed. Married women come home, see what's in bed and go to the fridge." Then, from the men's side: "Rule Number 1: Learn to work the toilet seat. You're a big girl. If it's up, put it down. You can handle it. We need it up, you need it down. You don't hear us complaining about you leaving it down." Or, "Rule Number 1: Men see in only sixteen colors, like Windows default settings. Peach, for example, is a fruit, not a color. Pumpkin is also a fruit. We have no idea what mauve is." And "Rule Number 1: You can either ask us to do something or tell us how you want it done. Not both. If you already know how to do it, just do it yourself." Such e-mails show that gender warfare, however spiced with humor, is alive and well.[27]

The danger of jokes is that they may seem to trivialize or overshadow the other parts of the sermon. When I preached the Galatians sermon, many more people commented to me afterward about the gender warfare jokes I told than about the body of the sermon. Did that mean they disregarded the main point or just that talking about jokes is more fun? I couldn't tell.

One of the most effective ways to employ humor in a sermon is to poke fun at yourself. Thomas Lynch, a funeral director and an internationally known essayist and poet, excels at self-deprecating humor. I heard him tell a version of the following story on two different occasions. He was in the bathroom when his son called from the hallway to say that *Time* magazine was on the phone. "It's about time," he said, reaching for the toilet paper. With his reputation and unusual perspective, they might want him to write an essay on undertaking or wish to interview him about his poetry. He finished his ablutions and scurried to the phone. "This is Thomas Lynch, how may I help you?" he asked with perfect courtesy. "This is Thomas Lynch, of Milford, Michigan?" the woman from *Time* said. "Yes, this is Thomas Lynch, how may I help you?" Still poised and courteous, he let an undertone of eagerness creep into his voice. "I'm calling from *Time* magazine today," the woman said, "to offer you a subscription at the special reduced rate of . . ." Laughter drowned out the rest of the sentence, and the audience was his.[28] Self-deprecating humor disarms our listeners and helps dismantle the pedestal on which we often stand.

Make 'Em Wait

When my father was in seminary, the wisdom about preaching was this: Tell 'em what you're gonna tell 'em; tell 'em; and tell 'em what you told 'em. This was classic deductive preaching. Later, inductive preachers disagreed: "If one's whole point has been stated in the introduction or fully made five minutes into the sermon, why should anybody continue to listen?" Fred Craddock said. "Time drags the sermon like a dead body toward the noon hour, and restless children are assured it will soon be over." Craddock urged preachers to use restraint instead so as to build anticipation within the sermon.[29] (More about building suspense later.) A friend of mine vividly recalled a sermon preached by Michael Lindvall using the Latin phrase *soli Deo gloria*. Not until the last minute did Lindvall translate the Latin for the congregation. "We were all in agonies of curiosity until the end of the sermon," my friend said. Suspense master Stephen King put it this way to a group of aspiring writers: "Make 'em scared, make 'em curious, make 'em wait." Thus our hooks should suggest, but not give away, the whole sermon.

Whether you open your sermon with a conflict, an unresolved event, a question, a vivid character, a strong statement, an arresting image, or a joke, a well-constructed hook is a form of pastoral care. We pay our parishioners the courtesy of engaging their attention before speaking of difficult matters. We honor them when we respect the fears, doubts, fatigue, or rebellion that almost kept them from worship. A good hook meets our congregations in their need and prepares them to go the next step of the sermon with us.

Try This

1. Study Your Openers

• Go back through some of the sermons you have preached and study your opening paragraphs. What kind of hook did you use? Did it express an idea or situation your people cared about? How closely did it relate to the rest of the sermon? How could it have been improved? Do you tend to use one kind of hook, or do you vary your opening strategy?

2. Identify These Hooks

• Go through the hooks listed below. What kind of hook is it? Why or how does it work?

a) "Can you blame the man? If the Jordan waters had sizzled when he stepped into the shallows it wouldn't have been surprising. And yet this man has always been on the list of classic examples of faith. Our Lord threw the name at the little stuffy dignitaries of Nazareth. Many lepers in Israel—but only Naaman the Syrian was cleansed."[30]

b) " 'Thy kingdom come, thy will be done, on earth as it is in heaven'? We pray every Sunday for God to bring in the kingdom of heaven, but I wonder if we really want it. Do we really want the kingdom of God to come?"[31]

c) "I am going to say a word, and the moment I say the word I want you to see a face, to recall a face and a name, someone who comes to your mind when I say the word. Are you ready? The word is 'bitter.' Bitter. Do you see a face? I see a face. I see the face of a farmer in western Oklahoma, riding a mortgaged tractor, burning gasoline purchased on credit, moving across rented land, rearranging the dust. Bitter."[32]

d) "Noah was a good man. I don't know exactly what that means to you. But it seems to me that when I meet good people my expectations rise, and one of the burdens of being a good man is, I suppose, that of living out our expectations of them. Noah was a good man. So good, in fact, that when the rest of the world seemed bent on self-destruction God couldn't stand the thought of losing Noah, too. Noah was a good man."[33]

e) "Well, here were are, just cleaning up the mess from Christmas, and ready to get on with life at a more normal pace, and we get this call to rise and shine. Rise and shine. The phrase reminds me of a story about a girl whose father, a regular early-riser, would peek his head in her bedroom door and call out, 'Rise and shine.' The girl would pull the covers even closer around her ears and mutter, 'I will rise, but I sure ain't gonna shine!' The call of the prophet to rise and shine doesn't immediately inspire us. We may rise up for the day, but we're not sure we want to put on a shiny face to do it. We don't want to be summoned for another job."[34]

f) "If there had been an inquest into Jesus' death, the parable of the two brothers would probably have been presented as one of the things that got him killed."[35]

• Compare these hooks, (a) and (b), for a sermon I wrote on John 3:1–17 about the beauty and terror of new birth in Christ. Which hook do you think is better? Why?

a) "You know, I've been remembering the day our daughter Barbara was born. Sunday, November 9, 1985. I remember driving along North Territorial Road on the way to the hospital. I remember how sun was pouring in through the windows but dark clouds were gathering in the west. (It was the week we got an early snow.) Feeling every pothole and breathing through the contractions, I was calm and scared, excited and fearful."

b) "On the day that our daughter Barbara was born, sun poured in through the windows of the car but dark clouds were gathering in the west. Breathing through the contractions, I could feel every pothole on North Territorial Road. Later, it would snow."

• Review the hooks in a collection of sermons by a renowned preacher such as Barbara Brown Taylor (*Home by Another Way*, 1999), Martin Luther King Jr. (*Strength to Love*, 1963), Fred Craddock (*The Cherry Log Sermons*, 2001), or Fleming Rutledge (*The Bible and the New York Times*, 1998). Or study an anthology of sermons such as *A Chorus of Witnesses: Model Sermons for Today's Preacher*, edited by Thomas G. Long and Cornelius Plantinga Jr. (1994), *Patterns of Preaching: A Sermon Sampler*, edited by Ronald J. Allen (1998), or *Those Preaching Women*, edited by Ella Pearson Mitchell (2004). Identify what kind of hook begins each sermon. Did it catch your attention? Why or how does it work?

For Further Study

Get a copy of the magazine *Poets and Writers*, and look at the column "Page One," which prints the first line of recently published novels, poems, and creative nonfiction. Which lines catch your attention, make you want to read more? What makes them work? How might the technique in these hooks be translated to preaching?

Chapter Two

Inspired Imagination

Cultivate Imagination

We all know preachers who seem perennially creative. Their stories are fresh and compelling, their language strong and vivid, their approach distinctive. I stand in awe of them. How do they do it? How do they produce interesting, dynamic, and original sermons week after week?

The most effective preachers seem to have unusual access to powers of the imagination. By "imagination" I mean the ability to enter deeply into the world of another, whether that person is a parishioner or a biblical character. Ralph W. Sockman said that imaginative empathy is very close to mercy, and often a prelude to prayer.[1]

An example: At the same time his wife was battling brain cancer, one of my colleagues landed in the hospital with severe chest pains. He said that finding himself wired to a heart monitor, and poked and pricked all night, as his wife had been for weeks, engendered in him "that sympathy of experience we call intercession." He described the experience "a simple twist of grace."[2] Likewise, Fred Craddock has recommended that preachers periodically engage in a "disciplined act of imagination" about their parishioners. Sketch a portrait of your parishioners in your mind as if they were strangers, Craddock suggested. Ponder their "names, faces, lives, relationships, addresses, problems, pleasures, and abilities."[3] Because so much of our work depends upon the good will of volunteers, we tend to narrow our perception of our parishioners to whether or not they like us, support us, or agree with us. Imagining them as if they were strangers helps expand our limited view.

I also found that visiting parishioners in their workplaces deepened my imaginative empathy. I sat with Jim, an insurance broker, in his twelfth-floor office overlooking a web of freeways. I saw a map of the world posted on the wall of Rebecca's cubby where she helped direct the installation of computer systems on four continents. When I told Tammy I wanted to see where she worked, she burst out laughing. "Somehow I just can't imagine you there," she said. Her tone of voice implied that because I was a pastor I had no clue about "real life." I had to strap on a yellow hard hat and clomp along behind her wearing toe protectors as we toured the chemical manufacturing plant where she worked. We dodged forklifts while she pointed out huge cylinders of toxic chemicals. Seeing the streaked windows in her office and the whiteboard list of projects marked "Done," I began to get a sense of the pressures and pleasures that occupied her days. The visits I made to parishioners' workplaces that summer changed my preaching. The questions and affirmations of the sermons had to connect to Tammy cutting deals with suppliers in her back office, and to Jim, and to Rebecca and others. Only when I had vividly imagined the world of my parishioners could I make a vital connection between their lives and the Bible.

Using imagination in preaching is not the same as making things up. Rather, imaginative preaching starts with the Scripture and tries to express as vividly as possible our experience of God's presence and power. Imagination is therefore an act of envisioning, an act through which we dream another way of being. Entering into the world of the Bible, we catch a glimpse of an alternate universe and see what our lives might look like under the subversive reign of God. We tremble with Isaiah amid smoke and fire and thunder in the throne room of God. We round the corner of a stone house and bump into an older brother who sulks outside while the sound of music and dancing vibrate around his younger brother within. We stand on a rocky shoreline of the island of Patmos alongside John, and we see with him 144,000 white-robed martyrs standing in ranks singing praises to the Lamb. Come, Lord Jesus!

The Dangerous Imagination

Yet cultivating the imagination may feel strange, even forbidden. Where will it take us? How far can we go? What is the relationship between inspiration and imagination? What comes from the shadowy places of our own psyches and what comes from God? Does God speak through the flights of our minds? These questions are hard to answer. Christian tradition has had an uneasy relationship with the imagination even though the church has relied on sculptors, painters, and architects to beautify sanctuaries and has asked musicians and poets to create the music of our faith. John Calvin warned against the imagination, asserting that people would worship not God but "a figment of their own brains instead."[4]

Since the Reformation, many Christian artists have suffered lack of support or outright censorship. A friend of mine, a potter, left her studio for campus chaplaincy, in part because she could not support herself on commissions paid by churches for her work. Madeleine L'Engle discovered the church's ambivalence about the imagination in a painful way when Wheaton College declined to accept her personal papers because certain donors to the school labeled her award-winning novel *Wrinkle in Time* as "New Age." Novelist Harold Fickett lamented that "there is a horde of self-appointed censors in the Christian community. The Christian business community has failed Christian writers. A lot of what happens in Christian publishing is a way to avoid real human experience."[5]

Churchgoers may have absorbed the assumptions of rational, pragmatic, utilitarian Western cultures, in which imagination is particularly suspect. Ambitious achievers are impatient with dreamers and loiterers, as columnist Russell Baker said in his autobiography, *Growing Up:*

> My idea of a perfect afternoon was lying in front of the radio re-reading my favorite Big Little Book, *Dick Tracy Meets Stooge Viller*. My mother despised inactivity. . . . "You've got no more gumption than a bump on a log," she said. "Get out in the kitchen and help your sister do those dirty dishes." My sister Doris, though two years younger than I, had enough gumption for a dozen people. . . . When she was only seven she could carry a piece of short-weighted cheese back to the A & P, threaten the manager with legal action, and come back triumphantly with the full quarter-pound we'd paid for and a few extra ounces thrown in for forgiveness. Doris could have made something of herself if she hadn't been a girl. . . . This must have saddened my mother, this twist of fate that had allocated all the gumption to the daughter and left her with a son who was content with Dick Tracy and Stooge Viller.[6]

My own mother, pressed by the demands of parsonage life, was always calling me from *Little Women* or a volume of fairy tales: "Get your nose out of that book and come help me." The church's ambivalence about the imagination has sent mixed signals to its artists, conveying the message that imagination itself cannot be trusted.

Some in the church may also fear that imagination will take us beyond the boundaries of orthodox teaching. Feminist theologians involved with the Re-Imagining Conference in 1993 experienced the depth and intensity of this fear. Persons who attended the conference lost jobs and funding, and the furor absorbed denominational meetings for several years. Guardians of church teaching want to preserve clear boundaries between fact and fiction, truth and falsehood, orthodoxy and heresy. Why risk misleading the faithful in order to indulge someone's flights of fancy?

Let Go of Control

Ambivalence about the imagination isn't just "out there" in the church. It is also inside of us, because releasing our imaginations requires letting go of control. Writing teacher Bonnie Friedman said, "The essence of writing is not control, but release. . . . When writing is going well it is not like pushing. It's like falling. You fall the way you do in dreams. You fall and fall. . . . We have an aversion to loss of control, as much as we love it. . . . We are terrified as much as we are enthralled by our own wildness. We don't know what will come out of it. We don't know what will come out of us."[7]

Several years ago my husband and I installed an electronic fence in our yard to keep our dog from getting loose. Sometimes I feel like I am the dog, so used to pacing the same perimeter that I stop before I get anywhere near the edge. I've forgotten how to venture into the great wide world, to roam the neighborhood, to sniff at things that interest me, to growl at threats both real and imagined, to greet other creatures with tail-wagging joy. I suspect that some in my congregation prefer me domesticated and contained. Yet certain wild passages of Scripture, like Ezekiel and the book of Revelation, read like unmoored imagination, far removed from ethical teaching or historical narrative. Inhabiting the canon alongside the stuffy pastoral letters and the lists of genealogies, they suggest there is more to faith than following rules. I long to follow Jesus, who was driven by the Holy Spirit into the wilderness to discern God's voice among the many voices, depending only on the sustenance of angels and the promises of God.

How do we release our imaginations without going too far? How do we keep from being seduced or overwhelmed by what we encounter when our imaginations lead? Calvin was right that any God-given aspect of our humanity can be corrupted. But I believe God is as interested in setting us free as in keeping us in check. Jesus, who spoke in perception-jarring parables and world-altering words, seemed as interested in breaking things apart as in keeping things in line. The Holy Spirit invites us to slip our leashes (not our collars) in order to imagine the world that is coming-to-be.

In the summer of 1994 I was stalled while writing a novel about a clergywoman who got in trouble with her congregation because she used feminine language for God. I went to a writing workshop lead by Janet Peery, hoping for help. While we sat outside in the warm, sage-scented evening, I told Peery I was afraid that writing the novel would get *me* in trouble. "I'm afraid my parishioners will misunderstand it," I told her. "I'm afraid my colleagues will be hostile. I'm afraid my superiors will chastise me." I ticked off all of the fears that were keeping me from writing. Peery was unsympathetic. "Then write it afraid," she said.

Write it afraid. That seems like good advice for preaching as well. We work in fear and trembling, respecting the authority of the church, yet letting our imaginations take us where our sermons need to go. We trust that the Holy Spirit is in the midst of the process, driving and correcting us, gently bringing us back when we wander too far. We can always return to what we have written, see what it says about ourselves and God, and ask the Holy Spirit to guide us as we decide what to say. Once we have preached, we can try to gauge the long-term results. "You will know them by their fruits," Matthew 7:16 tells us. We watch to see whether or not the products of our inspired imagination have helped our congregations grow in grace and truth.

With these cautions, I suggest three ways that we can cultivate our imaginative powers: praying, playing, and paying attention.

Pray for the Spirit

In the Gospel of John, Jesus promised: "The Advocate, the Holy Spirit, whom [God] will send in my name, will teach you everything, and remind you of all that I have said to you" (14:26). When the explosive power of the Holy Spirit was released at Pentecost, Peter stood up to preach. "This is what was spoken by the prophet Joel," Peter said. "'In the last days it will be, God declares, that I will pour out my Spirit upon all flesh'" (Acts 2:16–17). The same Spirit fires our preaching. Fred Craddock wrote: "It is unreasonable to believe that the Spirit was active in the writing and preserving of the canon and then abandoned the church that had to interpret these texts as a living voice to guide believers."[8] So, each time we preach, we pray for a fresh outpouring of the Spirit. The words of D. H. Lawrence beautifully express our role: "Not I, not I, but the wind that blows through me!" In Lawrence's words, we "yield" ourselves and are "borrowed" by the wind, which is the Holy Spirit moving through "the chaos of world."[9] Not only do we pray for the guidance of the Holy Spirit, but also we pray for those who will receive our sermons. One of my preaching professors told us how he prayed for the people in his first congregation. He divided the names in the church directory into groups of five or six and prayed for a group of names every day. He did not know many of them, but he prayed for them anyway. He told us that despite his inexperience it was the best year of his ministry.

Likewise, we ask our parishioners to pray for us. I love the prayer for the preacher from "God's Trombones," by James Weldon Johnson, which includes the petition, "Take him, Lord—this morning—Wash him with hyssop inside and out, Hang him up and drain him dry of sin."[10] There are many temptations that beset us while we are preparing our sermons and while we preach. We need the prayers of our people. Whether they employ Johnson's cadences, or pray in simpler ways, their intercession will help head off the difficulties and distractions that bedevil us, and will inspire us to be our best.

Play Around

Play! This second piece of advice may surprise preachers. Our work is serious, and we want to be faithful to God's will. Yet letting out our playful impulses can help us experience and communicate the gospel differently. When we loosen up and play, the Holy Spirit can tease out new ideas, prompt fresh associations, clarify complex thoughts, make new connections. When I am stuck in a sermon, sometimes all it takes to break the logjam inside me is a game of tug-of-war with the dog. (Other colleagues confess to secretive sessions of Sudoku online.) In her book *The Artist's Way*, Julia Cameron urged anyone whose work requires creativity to take a regular "Artist's Date," to do something that appeals to the child in each of us. The "date" could be a trip to an aquarium or museum or hardware store, a saunter through an outdoor market to linger over colorful fruits and vegetables, or a walk along a beach at sunset. "A little fun can go a long way toward making your work feel more like play," Cameron wrote. "We forget that the imagination-at-play is at the heart of all good work."[11]

We can learn from children and grandchildren simply how to see what is before us, wide-eyed and open-mouthed. Perhaps this is partly what Jesus meant when he said we must enter the kingdom like children.

Pay Attention

A third way to cultivate imagination is to pay closer attention to what goes on around us. When we first approach Scripture, for instance, we come not so much to look for answers but rather to let the texts speak for themselves. After reading the passage aloud and silently, we ask, "What's going on here? In me? In the text? In my people?" Pay attention to what strikes you, surprises you, troubles you, excites you. Do I like this text? Dislike it? Try to be quick, loose, fluid. Your reaction may not be "nice" or orthodox. That's good. Paul Scott Wilson said that "irritation can be a trustworthy guide" in studying the Scripture.[12] Getting to the place where the text begins to excite you or rub you the wrong way is a genuine starting place for preaching.

After noting our initial reactions, we can use any number of methods for deep exegetical study. We pay attention to historical, literary, and theological contexts. We note the meaning of key words or phrases or difficulties in translation. We explore other passages that the text calls to mind. We consider how form directs content. We summarize what the text wants to do and say. Literary critic Mieke Bal said these questions never fail her when she approaches a Bible passage: "Who is speaking? Who is seeing? Who is acting? And who is not doing any of those things?"[13] It is important, however, not to consult commentaries too early in the process. They should be used to correct or amplify rather than determine the direction of the flow of study. Trust your own questions. That is where your energy is.

Here is a study checklist that pays particular attention to the literary features of biblical passages, training us to look for those elements that translate most easily into compelling openings, suspenseful structure, and vivid language.

- Plot. What happens in the passage? What precedes and follows this action? List the verbs in the passage to get a clear picture of the action.
- Characters. Who are the characters in the passage? To whom is the passage addressed? With whom do you most identify? Least identify?
- Setting. What is the physical setting of the passage? Describe it with sensory detail. What objects are present or implied?
- Drama. What conflicts are present in the passage or implied in the situation? What does each character want? What is at stake? What is the outcome?
- Genre. What kind of writing is this (poetry, parable, proverb, narrative, rhetoric, etc.)? What effect does this kind of writing seek to have?
- Wordplay. What are key words or phrases? What do they mean?
- Audience. To what historical situations does this passage speak? What does the text want to do to or for its original hearers?
- Other works. What other Scripture passages does this passage evoke? What is the conversation among them?
- Reaction. In which of the above places do you connect most powerfully with the text? How might your hearers connect?
- Theme. To whom or to what situation does the text speak today?

Use a Journal

Another resource that can help us pay attention is the personal journal. A journal provides a safe, private place to record and reflect on what is happening inside and around us. The journal can be for the preacher what the sketchbook is for the painter, teaching us habits of observation. As pastors, we often see and hear things that are troubling or deeply moving. The thin arms of an elderly woman bruised by IV tubes. The break in a man's voice when he has given up on his marriage. Ashes marking the forehead of a young woman trying to break the cycle of anorexia. An infant in a white eyelet dress laid out in a tiny casket. Such things cause us to tremble. Writing in a journal can help us sort out the welter of our own feelings. Reuben Job emphasized the helpfulness of journal writing by including it as part of the daily discipline in his *Guide to Prayer for All Who Seek God*. In our journals, as Julia Cameron said, we can "sort through the differences between our *real* feelings, which are often secret, and our *official* feelings, those on the record for public display."[14]

We can also use a journal to record stories, quotes, insights, and great phrases we hear from others, like the comment made by one of my church history professors, "Jesus mastered the art of social climbing—downward," or the quip made by a radio disc jockey, "To every sport there is a season, and a game for every channel under heaven." One of my parishioners discovered for herself how helpful a journal could be. In March 2003, the room over her garage caught fire. No one was hurt, but there was so much damage from fire, smoke, and water that the house was declared a total loss. Church and community folk rallied around her family, bringing food and helping them pick through their belongings. During the process, Jennie kept a spiral notebook in which she wrote down important phone numbers and things they needed to do. But she also started a list of what she called "blessings," signs of God's grace in the midst of their disaster. She wrote down helpful circumstances that reduced the damage. She noted aid that came "at just the right time." The clincher on her list of "blessings" was a single sheet of paper found on the the grass of the back lawn on a Sunday morning. On the paper were two sentences her nine-year-old daughter had written the previous Christmas: *About Christ: Do you love me? Does this persuade you to believe me about Christ, that he was born in a manger on Christmas night?* Jennie believed that God was speaking directly to her grieving family through that salvaged piece of paper. With her family's permission, I used the story in a

Maundy Thursday sermon to say that God is with us in our suffering, providing signs of grace and power.

Had Jennie not recorded her list of blessings, I would not have been able to tell the congregation about it. And had I not written her story down shortly after she told me, I doubt I would have remembered the significant details. So many times after I've heard something powerful I've thought, "I'm sure I'll remember that." But after a few days, I forget. So, when you hear something compelling at a Bible study, a hospital bedside, a Rotary luncheon, wherever, get out your journal and write it down. If you don't have a journal, use a napkin, an envelope, the palm of your hand, whatever.

Just write it down.

Using a journal also helps the preacher clarify his or her own distinctive voice. Phillips Brooks said that preaching is "truth through personality." Though we preach one gospel, we each preach it in a unique way. Writing in a journal helps refine that combination of tone, vocabulary, and syntax that is as unmistakable as a fingerprint. Frederick Buechner told of a period in his life when he began arranging photos, marking possessions, taking stock. It wasn't just because he'd turned fifty, he said. "I had a growing feeling that, in terms of the mystery of faith, the place where God speaks—if he speaks anywhere—is in what happens to us. . . . I suppose my central message as both a preacher and novelist is 'Listen to your life.'"[15] Keeping a journal helps us listen.

Mary, the mother of Jesus, modeled the kind of attentiveness we seek. Susan VanZanten-Gallagher described Mary's example this way: "When the angel Gabriel showed up on her doorstop and said she was favored by God, Mary was much perplexed, and 'pondered' what sort of greeting this might be. Again, when her child was born during an unexpected journey to Bethlehem, and nomadic shepherds suddenly arrived at the stable with some outlandish story about angels, Mary 'treasured all these things and pondered them in her heart.' Twelve years later, Mary is still pondering, when Jesus disappears during a trip to Jerusalem and three days later he is discovered talking with the scholars in the temple."[16] Listen to your life.

Try This

• Write for ten minutes nonstop on "I remember . . ." Remember a childhood home, your parents, your first kiss, your first church, the day you were ordained, whatever. Write freely, sloppily, fast as you can. Don't worry about good grammar, complete sentences, or proper spelling. As writing coach Natalie Goldberg suggested, "Lose control. Every time you get stuck and feel you have nothing to say, write 'I remember' again and keep going. To begin with 'I remember' does not mean you have to write only about your past. Once you get going, follow your mind wherever it takes you. The memory can be something that happened five seconds ago."[17] If you get really stuck, write "This is a stupid assignment. I don't like it because . . ." Set a timer and do not stop until it goes off.

• If you keep a personal journal, set aside a day to go back through former entries. Highlight vivid phrases, powerful images, or recurring issues. Make an index of any entries that particularly capture your attention—they may be useful in preaching or teaching.

If you do not keep a journal, experiment with making daily entries for two weeks, writing longhand in a bound journal or typing on a computer. After a few weeks, go back and reread what you have written. If this is a discipline you would like to continue, set aside regular times for rereading and reflection, indexing entries by key words as you go.

For Further Study

Julia Cameron. *The Artist's Way: A Spiritual Path to Higher Creativity.* New York: Jeremy P. Tarcher/Putnam, 1992.

Charles Denison. *The Artist's Way of Preaching.* Louisville, KY: Westminster John Knox Press, 2006.

Book

Chapter Three

The Plot Thickens

Tell a Story

You've seen it happen. Members of your congregation sit in the pews with arms folded, shoulders slumped, eyes lowered. A woman buffs her nails. A teenager yawns audibly. But when you start to tell a story, people sit up. They uncross their arms and look straight at you. The woman puts down her emery board. The teenager stifles the yawn.

People love stories. When I was a child, my grandmother sent me a birthday card every year with a one-dollar bill inside. She always underlined the message on the card with blue ink and wrapped the bill in a piece of tissue paper. As June fourteenth approached, I checked the mailbox every day for my card. The year of my eleventh birthday, however, I lost the dollar bill. It simply disappeared. I checked the card, the envelope, and under the cushions of the chair where I had been sitting. I asked my mother if she'd seen it, and accused each of my siblings in turn of taking my dollar bill. I couldn't find it. Months later I pulled a book of fairy tales from my bedside bookshelf and opened it to "The Tinder Box," the story of a soldier who must get past a series of frightening dogs and other obstacles in order to gain wealth and win the hand of the princess. As I turned the pages to find out what happened to the soldier, there was my dollar bill!

Called to some chore, I must have put the bill inside the book to mark my place, closed the book, and forgotten it. I was elated to find it again. What I now know, however, is that the real treasure was not the tissue-wrapped dollar but the book of stories in which it was hidden.

Good stories help us understand what it means to be human. When we listen to a story, we imagine characters and identify with their conflicts. We inhabit their landscapes. We participate vicariously in their victories and defeats. Stories connect with us on a deep level, often in ways we do not fully understand. Listening to a story, our hearts may beat faster, we may hold our breath. Stories reach those deep regions of personality where perceptual grids are erected, self-image shaped, and hurts healed. From "Once upon a time" to "happily ever after," stories capture us and connect us to others.

Through his stories, Jesus drew people in, then turned their expectations upside down. Prodigals were heartened and the self-righteous unsettled. Jesus was heir to a long line of storytelling prophets. Nathan convicted King David of murder and adultery by telling him a story about a wealthy man who stole his neighbor's one ewe lamb to feed a guest (2 Sam. 12:1–15). Isaiah called the whole people of Israel to repentance with a story about a vineyard. He captured his hearers with a familiar scenario: "My beloved had a vineyard on a very fertile hill." Then, when the people passed judgment on the unfruitful vineyard, they passed judgment on themselves (Isa. 5:1–7).

After Jesus' resurrection, stories about him were passed from person to person, community to community. What he had said and done was told and retold, treasured, burnished, embellished. "For I handed on to you as of first importance what I in turn had received," the apostle Paul wrote (1 Cor. 15:3). Wherever the stories were told, people shared possessions, were healed of diseases, and risked persecution. Stories are sneaky. We enter their worlds, and find ourselves being changed.

Telling stories is more than a way to entertain distracted listeners. Story is the way faith happens. "I once was lost, I now am found" is a story. "Whom shall I send? Here I am, Lord, send me" is a story. "Christ has died, Christ is risen, Christ will come again" is a story. As Zan Holmes told a group of preachers, our task is to "tell God's story which is revealed in the Bible and the world in such a way that it *happens again* for both the congregation and the preacher."[1] Story is the very shape of faith.

The Shape of Plot

Therefore, sermons need to move as stories do. Whether or not they are "story sermons," they need to have a "plot," narrative movement, beginning to middle to end, a pulse that quickens as the sermon develops. As writer Tim Gautreaux explained, "Plot is not peculiar to short stories. It is not even a literary device. Plot is what interests humans in any type of endeavor. By plot I mean the entanglement of two conflicts, a development of those conflicts up to a climactic moment, and then some falling action. . . . That's the structure of a football game, a joke, a TV sitcom, of Shakespeare's plays. It's the structure of anything that engages human attention."[2]

The generic shape of plot can be diagramed as a mountain or a check mark. This shape is called "Freytag's pyramid" after the playwright, Gustav Freytag, who analyzed the structure of five-act tragedy in 1863 (see fig. 3.1).

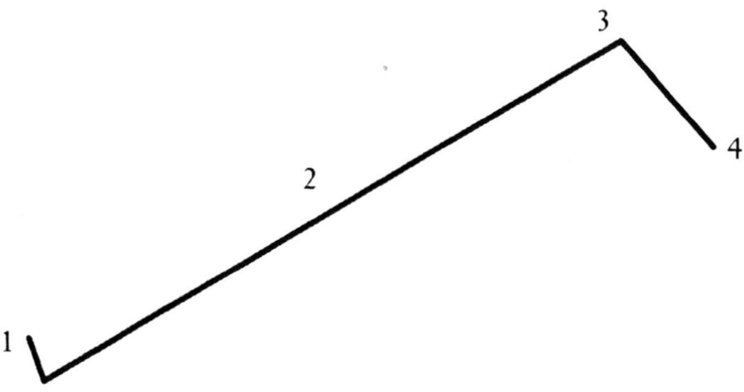

Figure 3.1. Freytag's pyramid

1. Hook: containing a conflict, question, dilemma, inciting incident
2. Complication: increasing difficulties or obstacles; also known as rising action
3. Climax: the point of greatest tension and emotional intensity when all the issues come together; also known as epiphany or revelation
4. Resolution: a way out of the dilemma prompting a change of perspective or some kind of decision; also known as denouement

Freytag's pyramid was widely accepted as a way of understanding plot structure in many kinds of fiction and drama. Novelist John Gardner refined Freytag's pyramid (also known as Fichte's curve) by incorporating little dips and rises within the whole pyramid to show the ascending emotional intensity within scenes, chapters, or sections of a novel.[3] These miniclimaxes lead to the final apex (see fig. 3.2).

Preacher Henry Mitchell said that "a sermon should be purposefully built on a pattern of ascending emotional intensity,"[4] which sounds very like the pyramid structure of plot. The traditional advice of black preachers also assumes the pyramid shape: "Start low, go slow; rise higher, catch fire." Eugene Lowry developed the

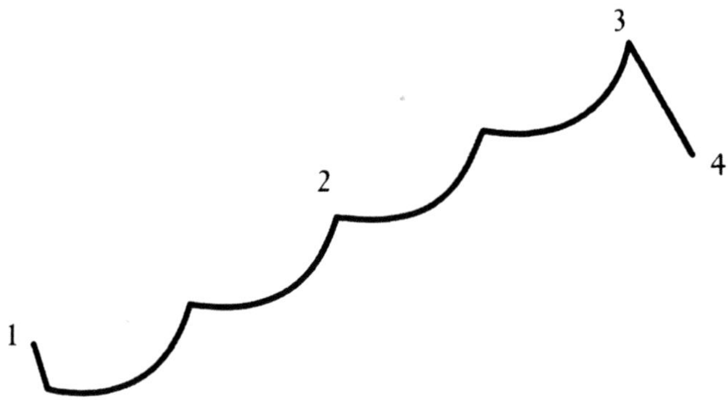

Figure 3.2. Gardner's version of Freytag's pyramid

notion of sermon plot even further. "A sermon is not a doctrinal lecture," Lowry said in *The Homiletical Plot*, "It is an *event-in-time*, a narrative art form more akin to a play or novel in shape than to a book. . . . Our best preaching does in fact feel like a story."[5] Lowry, however, described the shape of a sermon as an inverted loop rather than a pyramid. In Lowry's paradigm, a sermon moves through five stages: oops, ugh, aha, whee, and yeah (see fig. 3.3).

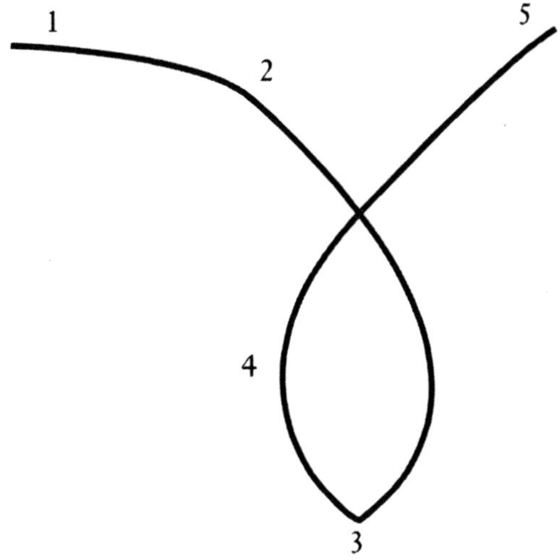

Figure 3.3. Lowry's loop

1. Oops: upsetting the equilibrium
2. Ugh: analyzing the discrepancy (diagnosis of the human situation)
3. Aha: disclosing the clue to resolution (a sudden illumination or reversal of expectation brought by the gospel)
4. Whee: experiencing the gospel (how the gospel addresses the human situation)
5. Yeah: anticipating the future (how life can now be lived)[6]

More recently, Lowry condensed his paradigm into four stages: conflict, complication, sudden shift, and unfolding, suggesting that stage 4, experiencing the gospel, could occur anyplace in the sermon. For Lowry, the shift, or reversal, is key, the moment in which the gospel speaks to the problem or ambiguity that opened the sermon, conveyed graphically by a turn in direction.[7] Lowry called the increasing intensity of the sermon "torque," a word suggesting deliberate application of pressure to produce rotation. What a wonderful image for conversion!

According to Lowry, the moment of peak emotional impact should not occur until just before the end of the sermon. "The congregation must experience aesthetically the utter futility of the search before the good news is addressed to the matter,"[8] he said. While the "turn" of a sermon is better represented by Lowry's loop, the idea of ascending emotional intensity is better conveyed by Freytag's pyramid. With either diagram, however, the important point is movement and pressure. Sermons need to have energy, to go somewhere, to do something. Perhaps you have heard sermons that seem flat or static, like scattershot around a central image or bump-bump-bump along a flat line, like beads on a string. Listeners say in frustration, "It didn't seem like the sermon was going anywhere." Plot is the means by which sermons move.

Make the Sermon Move

There are many classic sermon forms that build in intensity. In his book *Surviving the Sermon: A Guide for Those Who Have to Listen*, David Schlafer suggested three different strategies that can animate a sermon: image, story, or argument.[9] Some of my favorite sermon forms that generate suspense and move with increasing impact are listed by Fred Craddock in his book *Preaching:*

What is it? What is it worth? How can I get it?
Explore, explain, apply
Problem, solution
What it is not, what it is
Promise, fulfillment
Ambiguity, clarity

Not this, nor this, nor this, nor this, but this
The flashback (from present to past to present)
From the lesser to the greater.[10]

These forms generate suspense by arousing curiosity, thwarting expectations, or opposing different points of view. You can observe how the energy flows through them by rearranging the parts. For example, if you were to switch the order of "What it is not, what it is" to "What it is, what it is not," the tension evaporates. Why would anyone want to listen if we already know what "it" is? Putting the elements of the sermon in the wrong order is like telling a joke with the punch line first.

Henry Mitchell described several energetic sermon forms in his article "On Preaching to the Whole Person." He included the personality sketch, the dramatic monologue (a form more tricky than first appears), the dialogue sermon, and the figure sermon. In a figure sermon, an aspect of faith is compared to a common experience, such as running a race. Mitchell recalled a sermon in which he compared patience to the cooling system of an automobile. As he talked about the effects of loose head gaskets, frozen plugs, old hoses, and bad thermostats on vehicle performance, men in the congregation who usually sat listlessly were nodding vigorously.[11] (The danger in figure sermons, however, is in getting carried away. Limit the points of analogy to no more than four or the sermon gets tiresome.) Sermons can even incorporate lists, such as this example used by Carlyle Stewart III in a stewardship sermon. He characterized responses to the church's capital campaign as:

Cop-outs—who make excuses for why they can't give
Drop-outs—who leave when the church asks for money
Hold-outs—who need to be convinced
Fall-outs—who argue when the subject of money comes up
All-outs—who give generously when God calls.[12]

Though far from a story, such a list has cumulative power. The subtle humor of the wordplay helps lower the listeners' defenses.

They wonder, "Then what is faithful behavior?" The question builds in intensity as the list grows until the final phrase, "all-outs," provides the climactic answer.

Use a Refrain

Another classic preaching form utilizes the refrain, a trademark of black preaching. The refrain sermon by Martin Luther King Jr., "I Have a Dream," helped change a nation. A refrain provides listeners with "markers" to track through the sermon, and gathers new meaning each time the refrain is repeated. You can see how a refrain works by tuning into any country music station and paying attention to well-written lyrics. Tom Russell's chilling song, "The Sky Above, the Mud Below," a ballad about two horse thieves who cross a fallen deacon, illustrates powerfully how a refrain can heighten suspense and accumulate meaning.[13] The refrain structure is such a strong and versatile form that Fred Craddock wondered why it isn't used more often.[14]

Here is an example of how I used a refrain to weave together the opening of an Easter sermon, "Beyond Trembling":

> The waiting room smelled like disinfectant and stale cigarette smoke. The man across from Edith put his magazine down with a smack and went to the bathroom. Edith heard the toilet flush. The man came back and sat. He picked up the magazine and put it down again. "You want this?" he said. Edith shook her head. She didn't want to unclasp her hands. Five hours already in surgery. Quadruple bypass. His only hope, they said. When she reached into her purse for a butterscotch candy—his favorite, she kept them for him—she could hardly untwist the cellophane for the trembling in her hands. *Sometimes it causes me to tremble, tremble, tremble . . .*
>
> Patti was shaking all over. Part of it was the cold—it was October and her nightgown was too thin for the night air. But most of it was anger—How dare he? He'd been reading in bed as usual, one of his technical journals, while she was telling him how badly her boss had treated her that day, and

all he'd said was "Um-hum, Um-hum." Which led to their old argument—"You never listen to me" / "What do you want from me?" / "Maybe I should have married Robert" / "Maybe you should have"—until she'd pulled the journal from his hands and flung it on the floor, yelling, "I'm going for a drive, don't worry I'll be just fine." But she didn't have the keys, and when she went back after them, he'd locked her out. How dare he? The vinyl seat was cold through her nightgown. She hugged herself and continued to shake. *Sometimes it causes me to tremble . . .*

Though Greg did not know it, his legs were twitching in his sleep. All he knew was branches slapping in his face, the woods dark, the path twisting out of sight. "They" were after him. He was climbing, climbing, sliding on loose rock, trying to get away. He could not see their faces, but he could hear them, breathing hard, just behind him in the brush. His lungs were fire and his legs lead. He felt a rough hand grab his shoulder and . . . Greg's wife shook him and said, "Wake up, wake up," because he was sweating and the muscles of his thighs were shaking while he slept. *Sometimes it causes me to tremble . . .*

We all have known times of trembling when illness or anger or fear have set us shaking. We tremble at death, we tremble at the death of love, we tremble at the death of hope. At least part of what we look for on Easter morning is a way to stop the shaking in our bones.[15]

Try This

• Study the use of the refrain in Psalm 46, 80, or 136. Reflect on how the refrain works in each psalm. How does the refrain tie together disparate elements in the psalm or deepen the relationship between similar ideas?

• If one of your recent sermons has several paragraphs dealing with the same theme, consider how you might tie them together and accumulate emotional power by using a refrain. How might a refrain work in that context?

Mimic the Shape of Scripture

The biblical text itself may provide an energetic form for the sermon. Look at the structure of the passage. What does it do? How does it move? In many of Paul's letters, the underlying structure is problem-solution as he speaks to a question or issue troubling a church. Problem-solution, then, would be an appropriate form for the sermon. In Luke's Beatitudes, the structure is blessings and curses, full of tension between rich and poor, between humble and proud, between how things are and how they ought to be. A sermon composed of contrasts would mimic the text. Fred Craddock pointed out the "split story" form from the Gospel of Mark. In Mark 5:21–43, a leader in the synagogue begged Jesus to come and lay hands on his sick daughter. So Jesus set out for the leader's house. But before we find out if the little girl got healed, we're waylaid by another confrontation—the woman with the hemorrhage who touched Jesus' robe and stopped him in his tracks. Jesus healed the woman, and only then went on to raise the leader's child. Thwarting the hearer's immediate expectations adds tension and suspense to the story, Craddock said. But the form also reinforces the meaning: the woman was an interruption, yet Jesus healed her. The interplay of the two stories suggests that every daughter of God is worthy of healing. "Each story aids in interpreting the other while the arrangement provides drama and suspense. . . . What preacher would abandon that form in favor of some other?"[16]

When the biblical text is a story in its own right with plot, setting, characters, and dialogue, the preacher may choose to let the flow of the narrative be the shape of the sermon, trusting the story to do its own work. Some preachers like to add a few contemporary details that allow modern hearers to connect. I heard William Willimon do this once in a sermon, describing a biblical character who came into the house with two women wrapped in feather boas, one woman hanging on each of his arms. Other preachers tell the biblical story with contemporary characters, the story of the prodigal son and his brother being a perennial favorite. Such biblical stories need little embellishment—they almost tell themselves.

Alternate between Bible and World

Another set of energetic sermon forms comes from alternating between the biblical story and our contemporary situation, as described by Eugene Lowry in *How to Preach a Parable*. Lowry's book described three ways to accomplish that alternating movement:

> Delaying the story: beginning with a contemporary concern, then moving into the biblical story;[17]
>
> Suspending the story: beginning with the text, running into some kind of trouble in the text, then stepping outside it for more information;[18]
>
> Alternating the story: dividing the story line of the text into sections and interspersing it with contemporary material.[19]

Alternating movement adds drama and suspense, as well as establishing connection between biblical and contemporary worlds. The television series for children *Wishbone* used the same technique, intercutting scenes from a literary classic with scenes from a related plot set among contemporary youth.

A sermon on Genesis 32:22–31 provides an example of Lowry's "alternating the story" form:

Limping, but Blessed
Sondra B. Willobee

> Jacob is up against it. His twin brother, Esau, is waiting for him at the border with an armed company of four hundred men. It is payback for when Jacob cheated Esau of his birthright twenty years ago. Jacob prays a desperate prayer: "God, deliver me from the hand of my brother." Then he

comes up with this plan. He divides his company into two groups—oxen, donkeys, sheep, and slaves—thinking, "If Esau comes to one company and destroys it, then the company that is left will escape." Jacob also sends ahead a present for his brother, 220 goats, 220 sheep, 30 camels, 50 cows, and 20 donkeys. But Jacob himself stays at the very back with his wives and children. Will Esau plunder his possessions and kill Jacob and his family? Only morning will tell.

That night Jacob sends his wives and children across a small stream. He falls into a troubled sleep. Tossing on his pallet, he is haunted by the memory of his brother's face when he found out Jacob had cheated him of his blessing. Esau had cried out with a great and bitter cry. Hurt, disbelief, and fury had twisted his features. Turning over restlessly, Jacob hears again his mother's warning, "You must flee at once. Your brother is planning to kill you." Jacob's heart races as the darkness presses close around him.

All of a sudden, Jacob feels a man on his back. He's been ambushed! He flips over and wrestles the man to the ground. It is so dark he can make out no features, he can only hear the man's hoarse breathing and smell the man's sweat. "Who are you?" Jacob asks, but the only answer is the man lunging for his neck.

Sometimes, like Jacob, we battle difficult opponents. With what or with whom do you wrestle? Some of us have family members from whom we are estranged, of whom we are afraid, those who have hurt us and those whom we have hurt. Perhaps your adversary is cancer or Alzheimer's or Lou Gehrig's disease. A woman watched Alzheimer's slowly rob her of the mother she loved. First, it was the frustrating years when her mother knew she was slipping and couldn't help it, then it was the "easier" years when her mother didn't recognize her at all. When her mother died, the woman apologized for crying. "I thought I had cried all my tears," she said. "It's a horrid disease." Perhaps you find yourself pitted against a larger enemy—racism, sexism, war, terrorism.

Our struggle is even more complicated when it feels like

the enemy has a hold on our inner selves, as in depression or addiction. Jacob felt like he was fighting against his own nature. The conflict with his twin had shaped him since before they were born. Jacob came out of the womb holding tight to his brother's heel. "Is not he rightly named Jacob (which means 'supplanter')?" Esau said on the day Jacob cheated him. "He took away my birthright; and look, now he has taken away my blessing." At least part of what Jacob was facing that night alone by the stream of Jabbok was his own dark side. With what or with whom do you wrestle?

Jacob and his adversary struggle all night, the Scripture tells us. At daybreak, the man sees that he has not prevailed against Jacob, so he strikes him on the hip socket and Jacob's hip is put out of joint. Jacob grimaces in pain but does not loosen his hold, "I will not let you go unless you bless me." Good for Jacob! What courage and perseverance!

"You shall no longer be called Jacob, but Israel," the mysterious being says, "for you have striven with God and with humans." God! So is it God Jacob has been wrestling with all night long? Not his brother? Not his own nature? Not his own fears?

The ambiguity about the identity of Jacob's assailant in this story is deliberate. The narrator of the story wants us to wonder. The story expresses a deep truth: when we are in the midst of the struggle, often we don't know what we are battling—ourselves, another person, an evil force, or even God. The faces keep changing. The recurrence of the word "face" reinforces the same point: In the afternoon, Jacob says "I may appease Esau, and afterwards I shall see his face." At daybreak Jacob says, "I have seen God face to face, and yet my life is preserved." And when Jacob meets his brother the next day, Jacob says, "To see your face is like seeing the face of God." Jacob-Esau-God. Jacob-Esau-God. When we wrestle with our adversaries—our fears, our estrangements, and our own nature—we find ourselves face to face with God. Surprise! We have been ambushed! God is in the midst of the struggle, grappling with us, changing us, blessing us.

For Jacob is blessed. God keeps the promise made to Jacob before the struggle: "I will surely do you good, and make your offspring as the sand of the sea." Jacob becomes the father of the twelve tribes of Israel. His brother, whom he had feared so long, runs to meet him, embraces him, and falls upon his neck and kisses him. Jacob comes out of the struggle limping, but blessed.

Limping, but blessed. Actor Michael J. Fox, stricken with Parkinson's disease at thirty, described himself in much the same way. Sustained by a strong marriage, Fox worked through his fears about going public with his disease. In an interview with Oprah Winfrey, Fox described being at a benefit concert with his wife, Tracy, where a band they wanted to hear was playing. "During the early part of the evening," Fox said, "I was shaking badly and people were coming up to me, hugging me and looking at me with that look I recognize, and . . ."

"What look?" Oprah asked.

"They're looking for fear in me. When they don't see it, they then see their own fear reflected back at them. 'My God, could that happen to me?' I end up saying to them, 'You're going to be fine.' I want to tell them that bad things can happen to you and you don't know where they'll take you, and that is okay. . . . I've often referred to Parkinson's as the gift that keeps on taking. It's a gift in that it gave me a whole different appreciation for life. I have been enriched by what it has opened up for me. It hasn't allowed me to take anything for granted."[20] Fox entitled his recent memoir *A Lucky Man*. Limping, but blessed.

If the story of Jacob didn't tell us that God is in the midst of our struggle, grappling with us, changing us, blessing us, we would know it from the story of Jesus. Hymn writer Charles Wesley, one of the founders of the Methodist church, connected the mysterious being in the Jacob story with Jesus. Look with me at the hymn. It's number 387 in our red hymnbook. I'll lift out several stanzas:

Come, O thou Traveler unknown, whom still I hold, but
cannot see!
My company before is gone, and I am left alone with
thee;
with thee all night I mean to stay and wrestle till the
break of day.
I need not tell thee who I am, my misery and sin declare;
thyself hast called me by my name, look on thy hands
and read it there.
But who, I ask thee, who art thou? Tell me thy name,
and tell me now. . . .
Yield to me now—for I am weak but confident in self-
despair!
Speak to my heart, in blessing speak, be conquered by
my instant prayer:
speak, or thou never hence shalt move, and tell me if thy
name is Love.
'Tis Love! 'tis Love! thou diedst for me, I hear thy whisper in my heart.
The morning breaks, the shadows flee, pure Universal
Love thou art:
to me, to all, thy mercies move—thy nature, and thy
name is Love.[21]

Take heart. Love comes to meet us in the midst of our struggle, grappling with us, changing us, blessing us. Amen.

Look at the Big Picture

We can also preach a larger story structure within a book of the Bible or among a group of books. The Peter-Cornelius cycle in Acts 10:1–11:18, for example, spans more Scripture than can be read aloud in worship, but tells one story of how God sent visions to both Peter and Cornelius in order to open the Christian mission to Gentiles. In fact, the whole trajectory of Luke and Acts together can be preached. "Reading Luke-Acts as a continuous story enriches our understanding of both volumes," Robert Tannehill wrote in his two-volume study of Luke and Acts. "Promises of Jesus in Luke come to fulfillment in Acts, and our understanding of characters and events is deepened by suggestive comparison. For instance, Peter escapes from danger through denial in Luke but boldly confesses Jesus before the Sanhedrin in Acts, the contrasting behavior indicating the important change that has taken place."[22] The shape of the sermon does not need to be limited to bite-size pericopes. It's a big story. Sometimes we need to preach it that way.

Try This

• Go through an anthology of sermons such as *Patterns in Preaching: A Sermon Sampler*, edited by Ronald Allen. Study how the structure provides suspense and impact in each sermon.

• Review several sermons of your own and analyze the structure. How does the sermon move? Was the structure successful in creating the effect you desired? Were you conscious of using a particular form, or did you choose the structure instinctively? Do you vary your sermon forms, or use the same structure week after week?

Add Detail to Show Importance

There are other ways besides structure that we can build intensity throughout a sermon. In a story or novel, when a scene is important, the writer gives it more space and describes it in greater detail, signaling the reader, "This is important. Pay attention." Likewise, we can heighten impact by adding descriptive detail or by bringing the material closer to our hearers. We can also use pace, volume, inflection, and pauses to show the relative importance of the ideas we are presenting. Sometimes a whisper has more impact than a shout. Our strongest illustrations and our most eloquent language need to be reserved for the climax, however. This is not emotional manipulation. Rather, we are showing through the structure and with our voices that this is the most important part of the sermon, the payoff that demands their utmost attention. The same escalating intensity that pulses through the whole sermon can animate smaller units such as sections or paragraphs. The rise and fall of narrative is as natural as breathing.

Barbara Brown Taylor's post-Easter sermon "Blood of the Martyrs" provides a good example of how to use structure and detail to achieve ascending intensity. In the sermon, Taylor told several stories about martyrs for the faith, beginning with Dietrich Bonhoeffer, the German professor and pastor who was taken from leading worship and eventually hung by the Nazis on April 8, 1945. Widely venerated, Bonhoeffer was a good opening choice. However, the greatness of his reputation actually put him at some emotional distance from Taylor's congregation, as well as the fact that he lived in a very different time and place. "How could we possibly be like him?" Taylor's Georgia Episcopalians may have wondered. The next story Taylor told was about Jonathan Myrick Daniels, an Episcopalian seminary student killed while trying to protect a sixteen-year-old black girl in Hayneville, Alabama, in August 1965. This more detailed illustration increased the emotional intensity by coming closer to home for Taylor's hearers—their geographical region, their denominational affiliation, and for some, their lifetime.

When Taylor moved to her final illustration about Archbishop Oscar Romero, a Roman Catholic archbishop in El Salvador in the 1970s, she provided rich detail to characterize Romero and help him come alive for her listeners. Nonetheless, I wondered if she had erred in choosing as her closing hero a public figure in another country and culture. How will her hearers identify with Romero, and aspire to be like him? She handled this dilemma by characterizing him as a reluctant martyr. Romero began his priestly career as "an obedient chaplain to the military officers and wealthy landowners who controlled the country,"[23] Taylor said. He became a champion for the poor and oppressed only after he witnessed government soldiers opening fire upon a crowd. Most of her hearers could identify with Romero's reluctance, setting up her climactic exhortation: "Not everyone is called to be a martyr. Some of us try pretty hard to make sure we are not, but in these Great Fifty Days when we are working on what it means to be Easter people, I think it is important to remember some of those who believed it meant putting something ahead of their own safety."[24] By naming all of her hearers as "Easter people," Taylor placed them in the company of the martyrs she had named. Her final image brought the sermon inescapably into her hearers' own backyards: "What their murderers found out, over and over again, was that trying to get rid of them by killing them worked about as well as trying to get rid of dandelions by blowing on their puffs. The harder the wind blew, the further the seeds spread. Some of them blew all the way here."[25]

End by Going Back to the Beginning

We can end our sermons using many of the techniques with which we begin them: an image, a conflict, a question, a story from life, a memorable statement, a vivid character (see chap. 1). Taylor's image of the dandelion illustrates the effectiveness of using a strong or vivid image to close the sermon. Circling back to an image or phrase used earlier in a sermon can also be effective, and provides a satisfying sense of completeness. In a Maundy Thursday sermon on John 15:1–12, I began with an image of pruning a grape vine, quoting Phyllis Tickle's description of her husband at work in the grape arbor on their Tennessee farm. Attacking a wild vine ferociously, he chopped at the soil with his mattock long after the roots had been severed. Her husband did this, Tickle explained, because he wanted the juice from his grapes to be "perfect—translucent, pure ruby, and sweet."[26] Applying the image, I said that God hates the things that keep us from bearing fruit, and gave several examples of how God works in our lives to "prune" destructive habits and attitudes. At the close of the sermon, I held up a clear goblet filled with red grape juice. "When we allow ourselves to be pruned by God's word," I said, "Jesus himself is with us. The cup of blessing at our lips will be 'perfect, translucent, pure ruby, and sweet.'" The repetition of the phrase and the visual image of the juice brought the sermon full circle, and prepared the congregation to receive Holy Communion.

Not all sermon endings will be this tidy, nor should they be, but endings should at least resonate with earlier elements of the sermon. An ending can reprise a snippet of the melody if not the whole tune. Novelist John Gardner coached his writing students on what to do if the right ending eludes you. Reread what you have written so far, Gardner advised, and the work itself may show you what to do: "Read the story over and over . . . watching for subtle meanings, connections, accidental repetitions, psychological significance. Leave nothing—no slightest detail—unexamined; and when you discover implications in some image or event, oonch those implications toward the surface."[27] (Yes, he really wrote "oonch.") In this way, Gardner said, the piece will have a "resonant close" that stirs the reader. "What moves us is not just that characters, images and events get some form of recapitulation or recall: We are moved by the increasing connectedness of things, ultimately a connectedness of values."[28] A good ending will keep the sermon alive in the imaginations of the congregation and help move them on to the next step of faith.

Try This

• Go through the sermon "Limping, but Blessed" and note where the different phases of plot occur (hook, complication, climax, resolution).[29]

• The principle of ascending intensity applies to every unit within a sermon—sentence, paragraph, section, or whole. Rearrange the order of the clauses in the following examples to create a sense of ascending emotional intensity. (Think lesser to greater, farther away to close by, milder to more severe.)

> "Conflicts have a way of escalating, whether between (a) racial groups, (b) family members, or (c) nations."
>
> "Most of us know something about arguments getting out of

hand. We know what it's like to (a) catalog grudges, (b) plot revenge, (c) nurse hurts, (d) say something you regret later."

"Perhaps Paul remembered all that he had been forgiven: (a) his persecution of the church, (b) his unbending legalism, (c) his violent outbursts."

Once we have started paying attention to form, other kinds of writing may provide a structure for our sermons. Consider, for example, the collect prayer. This classic prayer form describes God and asks God to do something in response to our human predicament. The prayer moves through five stages: address (naming God); ascription (describing God and also implying something about human beings); petition (asking God for something); aspiration (the purpose of the request); christological conclusion (something about Jesus). The well-known "Collect for Purity" illustrates the form:

Almighty God, (address)
unto whom all hearts are open, all desires known,
and from whom no secrets are hid: (ascription)
Cleanse the thoughts of our hearts by the inspiration of
thy Holy Spirit, (petition)
that we may perfectly love thee and worthily magnify thy
holy name; (aspiration)
through Jesus Christ our Lord. Amen. (christological
conclusion)[30]

How might the elements of the collect form be expanded to provide structure for a sermon? Try it with 1 Thessalonians 1:1–7 or Mark 13:32–37. Look for the address, ascription, petition, aspiration, and christological conclusion stated or implied in the biblical passage. Use that movement as the outline for a sermon.

• The journalistic lead is another form that can help us in sermon writing. This durable format for the opening sentence of a hard news story has five **W's**—who, what, when, where, and why—and occasionally how. For example: "Federal regulators are threatening to take back millions of dollars meant to rebuild the Jeffries Homes, an aging housing complex, because the Detroit Housing Commission has failed to start construction after more than six years." The journalistic lead teaches us to look for what is happening in a biblical passage and to express it in simple language. Rewrite the main point of one or more of these passages in the form of a journalistic lead: Acts 2:1–18, Galatians 3:23–29, 1 John 5:6–9. Who is the primary actor? What has happened? Where? Why? How? This lead format trains us to be direct, concise, and comprehensive in the smaller units of our sermons.

For Further Study

Ronald J. Allen. *Patterns of Preaching: A Sermon Sampler*. St. Louis: Chalice Press, 1998.

Eugene L. Lowry. *The Homiletical Plot: The Sermon as Art Form*. Louisville, KY: Westminster John Knox Press, 2001.

Eugene L. Lowry. *How to Preach a Parable: Designs for Narrative Sermons*. Nashville: Abingdon Press, 1989.

Laurence Hull Stookey. *Let the Whole Church Say Amen! A Guide for Those Who Pray in Public*. Nashville: Abingdon Press, 2001.

Chapter Four

Finding Stories

Don't Settle for Prefab

It's late in the week. You have to finish the sermon today. You need something—a story, an example, an analogy, an image, something—to nail your point about the necessity of self-denial in the Christian life. It has to be good because it's the climax of the sermon. You've got everything else—a lively hook, clear and relevant exegesis, strong development of your theme. You think hard. Nothing. You get up and look out the window. Nothing. You leave your desk to get a cup of coffee. Still nothing. Is it time to go to "Sermonillustrations.com"?

Preachers use ideas and stories from other sources all of the time. A file folder of good stories is like a bag of gold. If you were to look in my office window on a Thursday morning, you might catch me shuffling through the clippings and notes I've collected, hefting their weight, assaying their value, like Midas fingering his coins. If my house were to catch on fire, I'd go back for the family photos and that file. One of my colleagues puts his collection of material in a three-tiered stacking file. He reads through them periodically, resorting them into the three compartments—good, better, best. Speaking to a group of preachers in Michigan, Tony Campolo acknowledged the reality that preachers are always looking for stories. He looked at us expectantly and said, "I asked a group of junior high boys at a camp, 'Can you tell me the difference between grace, justice, and mercy?' A kid says, 'Yeah, that's easy. If a cop pulls you over for speeding and gives you a ticket, that's justice. If he pulls you over and gives you a warning, that's mercy. And if he pulls you over and gives you a Krispy Kreme donut, that's grace.'"[1] After the laughter died down, Campolo flashed a wide grin. "Not bad. Write that down because you can use that." And we did.

It's tempting for hurried pastors to resort to "canned" illustrations from preaching books or the Internet. Resources abound. Pastors can subscribe to sermon services. Many denominational publishers offer preaching annuals. There are preaching Web sites and chat rooms. Many pastors post their sermons online. When I googled "sermon illustrations," more than three million entries came up. Some Internet stories circulate so widely that our parishioners have already heard them by the time we use them. The quality of such resources varies widely, though, and many "prefab" outlines and stories seem contrived. The biggest problem with resorting too quickly to others' resources, however, is that it short-circuits our own creative process. To cut and paste someone else's illustration may prevent us from pushing to the deepest level of our own analysis. We might never ask, "What does this mean to me?" or "Where have I seen this issue in my congregation or in the world?" There are some weeks when shortcuts are the best we can do, but it's a form of intellectual cheating if we consistently let others think for us.

Where do we find good stories and examples if we don't use prepackaged materials? What pastoral ethics and etiquette guide us when we use stories and examples in our sermons? And how do we incorporate them into our sermons so they don't sound contrived?

Read Widely for Quality Material

Sources of stories and ideas are all around us. During their workshop titled "Imaginative Reading for Creative Preaching," William Hulitt Gloer and Cornelius Plantinga Jr. urged preachers to read widely—fiction, history, biography, poetry, essays, children's literature, travel writing. The purpose of this kind of reading is not to "prettify" sermons or to sound more literate, Gloer said. Rather, it is to help the preacher see the things of God in human life, "grace in flesh and blood," to move the heart of the preacher so that the preacher can move the hearts of others.[2] Biography helps us understand human nature, and history provides evidence of where God is at work in human events. If we only read commentaries and church growth manuals, we will end up more like mechanics than pastors. We'll be able to adjust the throttle or swap out a belt in the church engine, but never step outside of the shop for a view of the sky.

An unexpected benefit of reading widely in good literature is simple enjoyment. When Gloer and Plantinga taught a three-week seminar on imaginative reading, they reported that by the fourth day of the seminar, participants looked five years younger. By the second week, ten years had dropped from their features.[3] One participant said that "the joy of the seminar was so prevalent that even the non-Calvinists among us began to feel vaguely guilty."[4] Because it may not produce immediate results, reading for pleasure can also help counteract what seminar participant Joel Kok called the "idolatry of success":

> As seminar participants discussed [*Remembering Denny*, by Calvin Trillin], we could hardly help but reflect on the extent to which success tempts us in our work of ministry. Could this idolatry be the source for much of our exhausting activism? Almost certainly it is. Many pastors suffer from what a friend of mine calls "justification by ministry." Such idolatry and such a false gospel make ministers feel too busy to do significant reading. They make ministry a joyless burden. They also promote miserable sermons.[5]

If reading time gets crunched by busy schedules, pastors can listen to audio books while driving in the car. (There's a danger in this, though—once a parishioner caught me in the parking lot of Botsford Hospital, motor running, while I listened to the end of a chapter.) A librarian, high school English teacher, or college professor can provide a bibliography of literature worth reading. The *New York Times Review of Books* is another source of worthy titles in a variety of fields. Sometimes the book that reopens our eyes will be on the bestseller list. Other times it will be tucked in a dusty corner of a used bookstore. The classics we were taught in high school or college are worth rereading for scope of theme, depth of characterization, and strength of story line. Preacher William Cotton said he likes to head to the library for an hour or so each week, pulling publications at random, purposely avoiding the religion section, looking for interesting images or unusual titles. Cotton found himself drawn to magazines about the physical sciences in 1988 when the Hubble telescope was conveying images back to earth. "The Hubble telescope with its powerful camera is providing a moveable feast," he said, "worlds beyond our imagination, as day by day it serves up an exegesis of Psalm 8."[6]

In my own preaching, I've used anecdotes from memoirs by Sue Monk Kidd and Anne Lamott; incidents from David Halberstam's powerful history of young Freedom Riders, *The Children*; a scene from Tennessee Williams's play *A Streetcar Named Desire*; portions of a short story by Tim Gautreaux; and stanzas of poetry by Gerard Manley Hopkins—just to name a few. In his book *Imagining a Sermon*, Thomas Troeger reflected upon a painting by Rembrandt in order to give flesh to his Christmas sermon on protecting human rights.[7] Once I described the panoramic view from the campground on top of a mountain at the Colorado National Monument in order to move into a sermon about Moses on the edge of the promised land. That illustration required me to read national park literature and travel guides. Students in my preaching classes compiled this list of sources for stories and illustrations:

- books, newspapers, magazines
- movies, radio shows, comedy sketches
- family life (everyday events, holidays, vacations)
- your own extended family history

- church history (your own congregation or the church universal)
- pastoral calls (ask people where they're from or couples how they met)
- mythology, folklore, storytellers' conventions
- rabbinic stories or tales from the desert mothers and fathers
- sermons, speeches, motivational speakers
- photographs, painting, art, architecure
- songs, hymns, carols, music videos, or YouTube

Some of the material you find may attach itself almost immediately to a particular text, as happened when I came across a citation of Abraham Lincoln's Fourth of July address in a book on speech writing. Lincoln had commented that while some American citizens are blood descendants from the original signers of the Declaration of Independence, others are newer arrivals. "When the [new arrivals] look through that old Declaration they find, 'We hold these truths to be self-evident, that all men are created equal,' and then they feel that the moral sentiment evidences their relation to those men, and that they have a right to claim it as though they were blood of the blood, and flesh of the flesh, of the men who wrote the Declaration, and so they are."[8] Lincoln's triumphant conclusion, "and so they are," seemed an exact parallel to the affirmation in Ephesians 2:19: "So then you are no longer strangers and aliens, but you are citizens with the saints and also members of the household of God." I copied the Lincoln excerpt and tabbed it to the Ephesians text.

If you choose your Scripture passages and plan your sermon topics in advance, you can drop ideas and stories into file folders when connections between your reading and upcoming sermons emerge. By doing this, your unconscious can begin to work on the sermon. Charles Denison compared this process to making "stone soup." Review the files periodically to "stir the soup," Denison suggested. "Each file, then, is a bowl of stone soup. We throw in a little cabbage, a bit of meat, a celery stick, a story, a dream, an article, a sermon we heard, a couple we counseled. . . .

We throw it in the file. We don't have to use it all. We may move some of it to another file if we don't use it now; some we will throw out as unusable. You want a fat file by Friday afternoon! That is the point."[9]

Acknowledge Your Sources

It should go without saying that we always acknowledge the sources from which our material comes. But some pastors do not. Perhaps they want it to seem that the ideas they cite originated with them. Or perhaps it feels clumsy to keep saying, "As so-and-so said . . ." A pastor of a large congregation in Charlotte, North Carolina, resigned from his church after a parishioner discovered he had been plagiarizing material from sermons broadcast on Christian radio. Another pastor in Charlotte discovered that a pastor in another state had preached all twenty-seven of his sermons on Mark without permission.[10] I once heard a pastor with a reputation as a great preacher tell a story from Fred Craddock as if it were his own. Give credit where credit is due. The damage to our credibility is incalculable when plagiarism is discovered. Astute parishioners are often able to tell when we are using material that does not originate with us, anyway. When I was pastoring my first church and feeling overwhelmed by its myriad demands, I used a large portion of a sermon someone else had written without paraphrasing it and without naming my source. "That didn't sound like you, Pastor," the organist told me after the service. Busted! I was so ashamed I resolved never to do it again. Even if we are never caught, we still have compromised our integrity.

With practice, sources can be acknowledged quickly and smoothly. The citation need not always take place at the beginning of the illustration. You may prefer to let the relationship of the illustration to the theme reveal itself as the story unfolds. However, you still need to give the congregation enough of a connection so they're not wondering, "And what does this have to do with anything?" Here are some examples of transitional phrases that help clarify the relationship of quoted material to the theme:

- "This description of a firestorm from a murder mystery by Nevada Barr almost makes you feel the flames of hell that the letter of James is talking about."
- "Rev. Ray Buckley, guest preacher at the 2004 Detroit Annual Conference, told how he learned forgiveness from his grandmother, a Christian and a Tlingit Indian from the clan of the killer whale."
- "Will you take the easy way or will you follow where God leads? A man named Bruton faced such a choice in the story 'Welding with Children,' told by Louisiana writer Tim Gautreaux."

When we use material from other sources, it helps to paraphrase it as much as possible, unless the wording of the original is crucial to our purpose. Putting source material into our own words helps us make it our own, and allows it to flow more smoothly with our ideas. I have to admit that I often resist paraphrasing, however. It's a lot of work, and sometimes I fall in love with how a particular writer speaks. I love the brash humor of Anne Lamott, for example, who said, "I thought such awful thoughts that I cannot even say them out loud because they would make Jesus want to drink gin straight out of the cat dish."[11] Or, I fall under the spell of the lyrical elegance of Frederick Buechner: "Someone we love dies, say. Some unforeseen act of kindness or cruelty touches the heart or makes the blood run cold. We fail a friend, or a friend fails us, and we are appalled at the capacity we all of us have for estranging the very people in our lives we need the most."[12] Some writers' sentences *should* be paraphrased, or at least broken up, because they are written more for the page than for the ear. I find Buechner to be one of these. (For more about sentence length, see chap. 6.)

When adapting material from novels, plays, or short-story collections, it is important not to let the quoted material take over the sermon unless it can bear the whole freight of your message. The more time you give to a story, the more important it will seem in relation to everything else in the sermon. In his book *Story Weaving*, Peter Morgan suggested that we wait a month after we've first heard a great story, to let it settle, to be able to assess its true value. "The powerful story to a public speaker is like steak before a hungry dog," Morgan said. "We who speak have a hard time resisting. What happens is that we become so eager to use a 'hot' story that we let it distort the text."[13]

Whatever material we use from others, we should respect the moral sensibility of our hearers. We want to be wary of illustrations that seem to glorify immoral behavior or employ questionable language. Sometimes, however, material that a scrupulous listener would find objectionable is absolutely necessary in order for the story to work. When I adapted Tim Gautreaux's short story "Welding with Children," I had to make a choice whether or not to use the phrase "bastard-mobile" from the story. I chose to use it verbatim because hearing that phrase used to describe his car shocked the protagonist into changing his life. I also kept another phrase that used a mild profanity, "Everything worth doing hurts like hell," because that phrase expressed the sermon's theme. It helped that the character in the story who said both of the questionable phrases was a Baptist layman. I tried to respect the congregation's sensibilities, however, by alerting them at the outset of the illustration with this statement: "Be prepared: the story has some strong language in it because it deals in hard truths."[14] You know your congregation best.

Motivate with Positive Examples

Stories that provide a positive example to emulate are more likely to motivate our hearers than negative examples to avoid. Several years ago I went on a mission trip to Tennessee with some of the youth of our church. One of the young men continually tested the adult leaders, brandishing power tools like weapons, clambering carelessly up ladders, stomping around a half-finished roof. His behavior provoked a constant stream of warnings and admonitions. Finally he said in exasperation, "Don't tell me what I can't do. Tell me what I can!" Also, don't use a negative example to make a positive point. I once heard a preacher tell about an outburst he witnessed at a funeral home where a family member told a would-be comforter, "You don't understand what I'm feeling." The preacher then said that God *does* understand what we are going through. God understands, but the funeral home story didn't prove his point. Sometimes, however, a positive and a negative image can be combined to great effect, as Jesus demonstrated in his parable about the two men who built houses, one on sand and one on rock.

Stories about extraordinary persons such as Mother Teresa, Mahatma Gandhi, or Martin Luther King Jr. usually work best coupled with illustrations related to people like those in your congregation. Otherwise, your hearers may dismiss your whole point, thinking, "Well, that was a great person; I'm just an ordinary Christian." I heard a fine example of this coupling technique in a sermon given by Bishop Hope Morgan Ward at the opening worship service of the 2006 International United Methodist Clergywomen's Consultation in Chicago. Halfway through the sermon Ward told a powerful story about meeting a woman in South Africa who had ninety-five orphan children living with her in her home outside of Cape Town. The African woman had started her ministry of hospitality thirty years before by taking in a friend of her young son. As years went on, she just kept adding rooms to her house. "I can't bear to see a child without a place to stay," the woman told Ward.

I was moved and inspired by Ward's description of the African woman's ministry, but it wasn't until the closing illustration that I was really convicted. In that story, Ward told how a church she had served in Raleigh, North Carolina, was part of a rotating shelter for the homeless. Unable to find a mission leader to attend a routine meeting of the shelter board, Ward sent a new member of her congregation to confirm the upcoming schedule. Ward got a call from the new member early the next morning. "I gotta see you right now," the new member said. Ward told her to come in to the office and braced herself for the woman's complaint. "We scheduled fifty-one weeks of the year, and nobody would take Christmas," the new member told Ward in great agitation. "So I stood up in the meeting and hit the table with my fist and said, 'I'm embarrassed to be in this room. We should all want Christmas.

And I tell you what. I go to a church that loves Jesus and we'll take Christmas every year.' "

"Oh, no," Ward thought. How would they get volunteers to staff the shelter during the busy holiday season? But to Ward's surprise, on the next Sunday the new member had filled her sign-up sheet before Ward even made it through the hand-shaking line. "We hosted Christmas for five wonderful years," Ward said. In the sixth year, Ward told us, the Baptists called. " 'It's not fair that you always get Christmas,' they said."[15] Had Bishop Ward only told the story of the South African woman, most of us in the auditorium would have let ourselves off the hook by saying, "That's not my situation." But all of us as pastors could identify with many aspects of Ward's second story—her wariness about this new member's agitation, her worry that volunteers wouldn't sign up, and her embarrassed joy that God had triumphed once again. The two stories worked together for maximum effect on her congregation of preachers.

Ditch the Inappropriate Illustration

Sometimes a great story is not the best illustration for a sermon. In the summer of 1994 I preached a sermon on Mark 14:3–9 focusing on Jesus' commendation of the woman who anointed him with oil. I loved the translation of the Jerusalem Bible, "She has done what was in her power to do" (v. 8) so I unpacked the Greek verb, *dunamai*, which means "to be able, to have power" the root of words like "dynamic" and "dynamite." Mentioning how Paul used the noun *dunamis* to describe the power from God that is at work in us through the Holy Spirit, I asked my listeners to think about what they had the power to do. I told of one man who had sent money for refugees in Rwanda and another who had become a surrogate father to a junior-high boy at Scout camp. A ministerial colleague had modeled openness with his congregation as he sought healing from depression. "God's power is often at work in unlikely ways that don't look powerful at all," I said.

Now it was time for the climactic story. Earlier that year I had read the powerful Civil War epic *The Oldest Living Confederate*

Widow Tells All, and a television series based on the novel had just aired. A certain scene from the novel would be a great ending to the sermon, I thought, so I set it up: "In this novel, one unlikely Rebel soldier does what he has the power to do." Willie Marsden had been shot in the leg. He was scheduled for treatment with the company doctor who preferred amputation over the tedious work of reconstructive surgery. Marsden begged his friend, Salvador Smith, to plead with the doctor for him. Just when the doctor called the nurse to bring the saw, Sal Smith burst into the tent holding two pistols like a highwayman in a melodrama. I then read directly from the novel:

> "Yes, Corporal?" asks the young doctor in the white gloves. "Have we been apprehended by our Northern brethren? The reason I mention it, you seem to be holding two dueling pistols aimed very much my way."
>
> "You've flat been 'apprehended,' sir. . . . It's a sloppy time, sir, and we're all taking shortcuts. But not on Willie Marsden here. No shortcuts on that leg. . . . Take as much care over this boy as you would during peacetime and if this was the President's boy and your whole life depended on it," Sal says. "Because sir? It does."[16]

I concluded the illustration with the sentence, "Sal Smith did what he had the power to do."

Serving as a guest preacher in several congregations that summer, I had a lot of fun with the sermon. In one church, I cocked my fingers like pistols with Sal Smith's question, "Because sir?" and the people said the next phrase out loud with me, "It does." Despite compliments about the sermon, I felt uneasy afterward. What was wrong? It was a woman in a low-slung black straw hat from a decaying neighborhood on the north side of Detroit who showed me what was wrong. "You surely blessed us this morning," she enthused in the hand-shaking line. "Now I know why the Lord had me come to church here today." She told me how a robber had come in when she was minding the store she owned in the neighborhood. She had pulled a gun from under the counter and the man ran away. A police officer to whom she related the incident approved. "I shouldn't tell you this," the police officer had said, "but your gun probably frightened him away." She adjusted the angle of her hat and smiled at me.

Near the close of the sermon, I had stated, "As Christians we cannot be pointing pistols at other people to get them to do what we think is right." But the woman in the low-slung hat hadn't heard me. She felt the sermon justified her action. She was right. The whole structure of the sermon, as well as the illustration itself, set up Sal Smith, the pistol-toting Rebel soldier, as a hero to be emulated. My one-sentence caveat could not withstand the momentum the sermon had built. If I believe in nonviolence, I cannot conclude a sermon with an illustration in which the hero achieves his "good" goals by using a gun. I had to ditch the illustration.

Create Your Own Story

However much gold we have hoarded in the form of good illustrations from others, often the most effective stories are those we tell from our own experience or the experiences of those we know. Some of us, like Bishop Ward, are natural storytellers. Others are not. How can we shape our stories so that our listeners are drawn in and convicted? The narrative structure discussed in chapter 3 can guide us as we create our own stories: hook, rising conflict, climax, resolution. In Bishop Ward's final story, for example, the hook was the problem of who should attend the scheduling meeting. The escalating conflict revolved around the new member's agitation and Ward's worry about the congregation's response to the new member's impulsive offer to host the homeless over Christmas. The climax was the moment in which every line on the sign-up sheet was filled. The resolution was the complaint by the Baptists that Ward's church was hogging the fun.

According to Michael E. Williams, editor of *The Storyteller's Companion* series, every story has setting, characters, objects, and action. Each of these elements can be used as springboards for the creation of our own stories. You can look for these elements within the Scripture passage or think about ways they are present in your life or the lives of the congregation. You may focus on the *setting:* When have I been out in the wilderness like the people of Israel, asking whether or not God cared about me? Or, you may relate to the *character* of a biblical person such Peter or Paul. So many of us have voiced Paul's lament, "I do not do the good I want, but the evil I do not want is what I do" (Rom. 7:19). Or, you may ask, When has an *object* conveyed a deep meaning for me? In the parable of the prodigal and his brother, the robe and the ring were meaningful objects. For a modern hearer, you might want to describe the new red Jaguar the younger brother got as a graduation gift compared to the older brother's used gray Camry. Or, if you wanted to stress *actions*, you could create comparisons and contrasts with the behavior described by Jesus in Matthew 7:9–10, "Is there anyone among you who, if your child asks for bread, will give a stone? Or if the child asks for a fish, will give a snake?" Persons who grew up in dysfunctional families may have experienced situations in which they did receive something akin to stones instead of bread, snakes instead of fish. Any one of the elements can launch us into a story.

As we weave these elements into our own stories, it is more effective if we are specific rather than general, and concrete rather than abstract. When describing an object, for example, it is more compelling to say "a one-eyed doll with a mohawk haircut" than "toy," or "a yellow Hummer with spinners" than "car." Choose distinctive details when describing a person, as John Updike did in his portrayal of a church elder in his novel *In the Beauty of the Lilies:* "the froglike, nimble, down-turned mouth of Harlan Dearholt, a small silk-ribbon millowner, whose short blunt nose supported a pince nez that gave off oval flashes of blind reflection."[17] Settings can be a as different as a played-out mining town in the Laurel Highlands of Pennsylvania or a gritty, mixed-race neighborhood on Detroit's west side. The more specific and unique each element is, the more authenticity your story will have. However, unlike the novelist, the preacher has time to include only those details that undergird the point. For example, to show that Mac Sledge was a wasted alcoholic, I only needed to report the whiskey bottle under the bedclothes and the missing wallet in his coat. The color of his hat and the shape of his belt buckle were not significant. Too much description will weary and sidetrack our listeners.

Use Dialogue to Convey Character and Action

Incorporating dialogue into our stories gives them the feel of real life, and reveals character more quickly than description. To create authentic dialogue, listen to how people really talk. Write down snippets of conversations you overhear in restaurants, at sporting events, or at the mall. Fiction editors Renni Brown and Dave King suggested that writers resist the urge to explain what characters say with phrases such as "He said in astonishment" or "She said primly." Instead, let the dialogue speak for itself. They also advised against using substitutions for "said" such as "he chuckled" or "she grimaced." Explanatory words such as these actually detract from the dialogue.[18] A preacher can eliminate some "saids" altogether by changing head position to show a change in speaker.

The following fictional scene shows how dialogue can set forth a conflict and reveal character. It was the opening for a sermon on Luke 4:14–21 that focused on listening for and accepting our commissions from God.

> Thanksgiving dinner. There was only a scraping of mashed potatoes left in the bowl, a dribble of gravy on the tablecloth, the skeleton of the turkey in the kitchen. The father looked at the wreck of the table and said with a satisfied sigh, "That was *good*." Everyone else around the table nodded happily. It was then that the oldest son, a political science major at U of M, dropped the bombshell. "I've decided to change my major," he said. "I'm entering the School of Art. I want to become a potter." The father drew in his breath sharply, as if he'd been sucker-punched. The mother looked aghast. "We've talked for years about you being a lawyer like your father," she said. "You spent all those summers clerking for

> him, the two of you coming home together, talking about clients, and how you could fit into the firm one day."
>
> "Yes, and remember what I did once I was home, Mom? I went down to the basement to my wheel and threw a pot. I took classes at the Art Institute, and my *Spirit Heart* won second place in a juried show."
>
> "We're glad you have outside interests, dear, that's why we bought you the potter's wheel in the first place," the mother said. "We want you to be a happy, well-rounded . . ."
>
> "Pottery is a hobby, not a job," the father said. "A. Income is minuscule and sporadic. B. No health insurance. C. No one values pottery as a career. Tourists may buy a vase or a mug from a shop while they're vacationing in Traverse City, but throwing pots is not a life. If it were, potters would make millions and corporate lawyers would set up booths at art shows."
>
> "Ridicule me all you want, Dad, but my mind is made up. I feel as if God has given me a gift, a calling. Not to listen would be to throw it back in his face."
>
> "Don't bring God into this, young man. As if God wanted you to be destitute and despised. Get it through your head—there's a lot of things I'm willing to do with my money, but supporting a starving artist isn't one of them."[19]

I hoped that the use of dialogue would draw my listeners in, move the story along, and help them identify with the characters. After this scene, I moved into a paragraph describing how Jesus had taken a commission from God that offended his family and friends.

Try This

Tell an experience from your youth or childhood—fighting with a bully, rescuing an animal, creating a secret hideaway, being lost from parents, moving to a new place, surviving an outdoor adventure, beginning a new year of school, going on your first date. Be sure to incorporate setting, characters, objects, and action/conflict.

Feel free to include dialogue. You may tell the story in your own voice (first person) or as if it happened to someone else (third person).

Slant the Story to Express the Theme

My colleague and I were attending a luncheon after a funeral service for a church member. The restaurant was not ready when we arrived, so we sat for nearly half an hour, drinking coffee, chewing ice cubes, and fidgeting with the linen tablecloths. "Bob," a distant relative of the deceased, sat across from us. Seeing he had the undivided attention of two pastors, he said, "Can I tell you something?" and launched into a monologue:

> Before I tell you this story, and I've only told one other person (nodding toward his fiancée), I want you to know that I'm a computer manager, and I believe in science. It happened to me six years ago, and I'm still trying to make sense of it, to analyze it, to know what happened.
>
> I woke up in the middle of the night with a sense of cold beside me, an evil presence. Then I felt intense pain in my heart, as if someone had taken it and put it in a vise. I know it wasn't a dream because I was awake and felt these sensations. I don't know where the words came from, but I found myself saying, "Help me, Jesus."
>
> Instantly there was a flash like lightning that hit my heart, white light all around me, and I saw a face on the wall. It didn't look like any of the pictures in the books or in paintings, but I knew it was Jesus. Then I had the strangest sensation of complete calm. I wasn't worrying about bills or parents or anything. I was just *there*—and happy. And you know how even in the middle of the night you usually hear something in the house, like the floor creaking or the refrigerator coming on? There was no sound. Absolute silence. I was calm.
>
> Then I had the sensation of falling—crash—down onto my bed. And I was glad to be there, you know, like I wasn't dead, but I also wanted to be back where that calm feeling was.

> I found out several years later that I have a damaged heart. There is scar tissue on my heart. I've been trying to figure out what happened. Did I have a heart attack? It wasn't like the near-death experiences that you read about; there was no dark tunnel or flashing lights, just this white light all around me. Other people might say it was my subconscious kicking in when I said, "Help me, Jesus." What do you think?

He sat back and looked at us. We talked to him about different ways the experience could be interpreted, but told him our conviction that he had, indeed, experienced a miraculous healing.

In what kind of sermon would you use Bob's story? It could be preached as a healing story, as a conflict-of-cosmology story (science vs. religion), as a story about confrontation with evil, or in many other ways. My colleague, who got to the pulpit first, used it on Easter as a story of resurrection. The context and purpose of a story will shape how we tell it, what details to emphasize, and what to omit.

Try This

Choose one or more of the angles suggested in the paragraph above and shape Bob's story to that theme. Write a transition sentence to introduce the story as well.

Always Ask Permission

When telling stories that involve persons other than ourselves, we need to respect confidentiality. Ask permission ahead of time if you name names or retain significant identifying details. Even if the incident was public or is known to members in the congregation, you may still want to check with persons involved. It is one thing to tell one's experiences to a Bible study class or a fellowship group; it is quite another to hear your story spoken to the whole congregation on Sunday morning. Preachers can also protect confidentiality by making a composite of characters and events, changing enough details to mask identity.

Pastors' families often bear the burden of being the subject of sermon illustrations. When my children were little, I bought them off by agreeing to pay them twenty-five cents every time I mentioned them in a sermon. When they got older, the price went up to a dollar. Besides annoying the people you love best, the danger of telling family stories is that congregants may get sidetracked into speculating about the state of the pastor's home life rather than the message of the sermon. In any case, the same rule applies with family members as with parishioners: ask first.

It's Not about You

What about telling stories in which we are the primary subject? I recall the hushed, electric silence in the auditorium when a clergy colleague, the recipient of an evangelism award, told how he had been rescued from drug addiction by the grace of God and the perseverance of his own pastor. Testimonies of how God has saved persons from sin and addiction are tremendously powerful. When we tell stories from our own lives, we need to be clear that the story is for the sake of the sermon and not for ourselves. Walter Wangerin advised a group of pastors, "the community must justify the telling of the story." This is sometimes a tricky discernment to make, because even berating ourselves can subtly shift the focus to us. Wangerin also cautioned that we should use stories that talk about our own sin only after we've repented and received forgiveness.[20] Our story should provide enough information to suggest the shape of sin without divulging details that would titillate or embarrass our hearers.

The language and content of the penitential psalms (6, 32, 38, 51, 102, 130, 143) may help us with the proper tone of confessional materials. In these psalms, the most vivid language is reserved not for description of the sinful acts but for the psalmist's remorse: "Be gracious to me, O LORD, for I am languishing; O LORD, heal me, for my bones are shaking with terror. I am weary with my moaning; every night I flood my bed with tears" (Ps. 6:2, 6). When we tell stories of our own suffering or wrongdoing, we must have enough emotional distance from personal material not to break down in the telling. Otherwise the congregation will remember only that we "lost it" rather than the message of the sermon.

We pastors need regular conversation with our own mentors and spiritual directors to keep our preaching free of inappropriate disclosure or self-aggrandizement. The pulpit should not be our confessional. Leander Keck demonstrated how one can speak effectively about one's own weakness in his sermon on Mark 6:30–44. He said, "I recall preaching a sermon so weak that I wished I could have sneaked out the back way. But at the door, a person who seldom commented made it a point to say my sermon had been helpful. To this day I can't see what it could have been that helped her, but one of my little loaves was blessed and she was fed."[21] Keck whittled himself down to the right size and saved himself from being the hero of this story with the phrases "so weak" and "can't see what" and "little loaves." In Keck's example, the focus was on God's provision rather than on the preacher's power. As Scottish theologian James Denny said, "No preacher can both convince a crowd that he is clever and that Jesus Christ is mighty to save."[22]

Try This

Read the following personal story that I used to conclude "Unrolling the Scroll," the sermon on Luke 4:14–21 about accepting our commissions from God. Do you think the story successfully avoided inappropriate disclosure or self-aggrandizement by the preacher? Why or why not?

> Maybe some of you think that because I'm a pastor I'm always clear about and eager to do what God wants me to do. NOT. Back me up on this, other pastors in the congregation—sometimes people in the religion business just get better at resisting God with righteous-sounding reasons. Anyway, the thought had kept coming up in my mind (and that's one of the ways God speaks to us, through thoughts that keep coming up in our minds) that we need to do more hands-on mission work here at Farmington First. But when

a colleague described her Volunteer in Mission trip to help build a school in Liberia, I shook my head. I'm already working too many hours, I said to myself. When I saw a cover story in *The Michigan Christian Advocate* about a mission team going to New Orleans, I turned the magazine face down on the coffee table. Outreach is someone else's responsibility—it's outside my job description. When I thought about my week in Appalachia with the youth several years ago, my stomach clenched. Our crew was working on a roof, and we didn't tarp it properly when we left the site, and it rained overnight, torrential rain. Our family unplugged the fuse box because they were afraid of it shorting out and they sat in the dark with rain pouring into their house. Don't ask me to go, God, I'll screw it up.

Well, last March our daughter Barbara went down to Biloxi, Mississippi, with a campus ministry group to help clean up after Hurricane Katrina. The next time we saw her, there was light in her eyes and energy in all of her limbs. "I want to go back to Mississippi," she said. "And I want my church to go." My church. Us. OK, God, I said. I unrolled the scroll. And look what God did. Fourteen people went to Ocean Springs, Mississippi, the first week of January and eleven more will go February 17. Any member of the team could tell you how bountifully God provided during our week of work, how freely the Holy Spirit flowed. It was fun! We laughed, we teased each other, we came to each other's aid. One person steadied the ladder while another one climbed. It wasn't just about painting walls or pulling up floors. We were trying to be, in the words of the site coordinator, "Jesus with skin on."[23]

Make It Up

We can also tell stories that are entirely fictional, the product of our own observations and imagination. As Ronald Allen pointed out in *Preaching: An Essential Guide*, "The Bible contains stories that are obviously made up," such as Jesus' parables or the prophet Nathan's story of the theft of the ewe lamb.[24] You can clue your listeners that the story is fictional with a phrase like "Once there was" or "A certain man." Fables or allegories are other examples of fictional stories, such as Martin Bell's "Barrington Bunny,"[25] or Walter Wangerin's story "Lily."[26] An implausible detail, such as talking animals or a beanstalk growing up into the sky, will demonstrate that the story takes place in the border between reality and fantasy. In fiction, this in-between genre is called "magic realism," a kind of literature in which magical elements occur in an otherwise realistic setting.

Fred Craddock told a story in the form of "magic realism" to conclude a sermon on Matthew 13:24–30, "But What about the Weeds?" Visiting in the home of a family he knew, Craddock watched their adopted racing dog as it lay on the floor in the den. A toddler pulled on its tail and an older child used its stomach for a pillow. Craddock asked the dog why it had quit racing. "Were you mistreated?" he asked. "No." Were you worn out, or luckless, or crippled, he wondered. "No," the dog said. "But why did you quit?" Craddock said. "I discovered that what I was chasing was not really a rabbit," the dog told him. "All that running and running and running and running, and what was I chasing? It wasn't even real."[27] Craddock used the story to drive home his point that people can change, so that we should not presume to say what God will do with them. Though the talking dog was clearly a fiction, the setting and dialogue had enough verisimilitude that the story was convincing. Eugene Lowry once said of Craddock that he "thinks weird." Sometimes a preacher has to loosen up, let go, or be outrageous, ridiculous, deliberately deceitful, in order to discover where an illustration needs to go.

There is a similarly "weird" imagination at work in the preaching of Debbie Blue, pastor of House of Mercy Church in St. Paul, Minnesota. Retelling the parable of the Laborers in the Vineyard, Blue described the mid-morning workers as the kind of people who had Cheerios or Pop-Tarts for breakfast "on the way out the door and they didn't brush their teeth." The people hired a little later "crawled out of bed at eleven and were on their way to get a paper (or more like a hot rod magazine or a TV guide) and a donut or a big greasy bacon breakfast. And then they were planning to go back to their couch and watch daytime TV." She described one of the workers hired last as "some guy who just woke up, puked, kicked his dog, and left his house to start drinking again."[28] Blue's descriptions of fictional characters delivered the full shock of the parable. Make it up.

Try This

• Write about a recent incident you witnessed. Use your own voice. Then rewrite it in third person and change several significant details. Does the story want to go somewhere else? Is the emotional core of the experience the same? Let the revised story become "the lie that tells the truth."

• Go to a public library and read the first pages of these novels, which are written in the genre of magic realism: *Like Water for Chocolate*, by Laura Esquivel; *One Hundred Years of Solitude*, by Gabriel García Márquez; *The House of Spirits*, by Isabel Allende. What elements of the story are fantastic or magical? What elements of the setting are realistic? Note the richness of sensory details, the use of symbolism and imagery, the way in which characters accept the fantastical elements of the story without question. How might these techniques be used to create a sermon illustration?

• Write about an important person in your life—a relative, mentor, friend. Frederick Buechner described several beloved characters in his memoir *The Sacred Journey*—his "fierce and terrified" grandmother and his prep-school teacher, a man with "a tremendous Irishman's zest for the blarney and wizardry of words." Buechner concluded his character sketches with this admonition: "On All Saints' Day, it is not just the saints of the church that we should remember in our prayers, but all the foolish ones and wise ones, the shy ones and overbearing ones, the broken ones and whole ones, the despots and tosspots and crackpots of our lives who, one way or another, have been our particular fathers and mothers and saints, and whom we loved without knowing we loved them and by whom we were helped to whatever little we may have, or hope to have, of some kind of seedy sainthood of our own."[29] Prompted by Buechner, I wrote a paragraph about my eighth-grade English teacher:

> Mrs. Goosey would not have been called a saint by anyone, but particularly not by members of the school board, who disapproved her politics and her clothes. A thin, bony woman with a broad forehead and lank red hair, she wore the wild fashions of the day, short, straight skirts in eye-popping combinations of deep purple and hot pink. She read to us from E. E. Cummings, Robert Frost, and World War II poet Siegfried Sassoon, whose bitter verses mounted an opposition to the current war we watched every night on our television screens. We talked in class about heroes, about our country, and about values. Through the passion in her voice we got a glimpse of what words could do. Though she had an outlandish wardrobe and a ridiculous name, June Goosey helped shape my mind and cast the direction of my life. She was one of my "saints."[30]

Describe one of your "saints."

For Further Study

Creating Fiction: Instruction and Insights from Teachers of the Associated Writing Programs. Edited by Julie Checkoway. Cincinnati, OH: Story Press, 1999.

Stone

Chapter Five

Language of the Incarnation

Use Concrete Language to Convey Religious Experience

It's a fist-size chunk of gray granite, oblong, dusted with rose quartz. When I hold it in my palm, my fingers curve around it, my thumb finding an indentation on one side. The stone is heavy and cool, the surface rough. The heft of it makes me think of stones along the roads in Jerusalem, the stones Jesus said would cry out if his followers were silenced, the weapons of Palestinian youth during the intifada. According to the *Golden Guide to Rocks and Minerals*, this piece of granite is an igneous rock, formed from magma deep below the surface of the earth. I found it along the Huron River in southeastern Michigan and took it home to edge the birdbath in our garden. Now, however, it sits on top of the bookshelf opposite my computer. My eyes fall on it several times a day.

Why do I keep a rock within view of my computer? To hurl at the monitor when my hard drive crashes? (Not if, but when.) No, the rock is to remind me to stay grounded in the tangible world while I work. Because of the nature of ministry, I do most of my communicating in what Philip Wheelwright called "steno-language." Steno-language is the language of logic and definition, the language of business letters, scholarly articles, and management journals. It relies on abstract, multi-syllable words like "ecclesiology" and "facilitation." Steno-language enables us to communicate precisely and efficiently, but it does not express all of human experience. A different kind of language is needed to communicate religious experience, Wheelwright said: "depth" or "expressive" language. Depth language has a softer focus, relying on imagery to convey multiple layers of meaning. With depth language, several conflicting things can be true at the same time. Depth language tries to evoke the otherness just beyond ordinary perceptions of reality. It is the language of transcendence.[1] Poet Kathleen Norris called it "incarnational language"—"ordinary words that resonate with the senses as they aim for the stars."[2]

The prophet Isaiah used incarnational language when he wanted to express what it means to be human. Rather than saying, "People are perishable," he said, "All flesh is grass" (Isa. 40:6, KJV). Likewise, when the psalmist wanted to talk about our relationship to God, he didn't say, "What value can human beings possibly have in the cosmos?" He said, "When I look at your heavens, the work of your fingers, the moon and the stars that you have established; what are human beings that you are mindful of them?" (Ps. 8:3–4). Notice how many of the biblical words evoke one or more of the senses to express a deeper meaning: flesh, grass, moon, stars, fingers. The poet Emily Dickinson said that she studied the Bible to learn "the mode of juxtaposing elements of concrete things with equally fundamental ideas and feelings—grass, stone, heart, majesty, despair."[3]

Biblical writers used many different kinds of depth language to convey religious experience. Some of their expressive language included figures of speech such as simile, paradox, personification, and metaphor. "Like vinegar on a wound is one who sings songs to a heavy heart," the writer of the Proverbs said. "Satan desired to have you, that he may sift you as wheat," Jesus told his disciples. Both of these are examples of *simile*, simple comparisons that use "like" or "as." When Jesus said, "Blessed are the poor," he was speaking in *paradox*, saying conflicting things at the same time. Other biblical writers used the device of *personification* to express a religious truth. "The mountains skip like rams, the trees clap their hands," the psalmist said. Personification gives a human attribute to a natural force or object.

A more complex comparison that says one thing in terms of another is called a *metaphor*. According to Mennonite poet Julia Kasdorf, a metaphor is a bridge between the known and unknown, a "temporary coupling of unlike things" that suggests new meaning.[4] Jesus was a master of metaphor. "Give, and it will be given to you. A good measure, pressed down, shaken together, running over, will be put into your lap; for the measure you give will be the measure you get back" (Luke 6:38). Jesus compared the kingdom of God to the growth of a mustard seed, ten bridesmaids with oil lamps, a ruler who summoned his slaves before going on a journey. "The natural object is always the adequate symbol," Kasdorf said. "It is the quickest way to express inarticulate feelings or confounding experience."[5]

The depth language of the Bible is not simply decorative. It wants to bring about the experience or the change it describes. "The poetic language of Jeremiah is not just a skillful or occasional cloak for an eternal word," biblical scholar Walter Brueggemann said. "It is part of the strategy for letting the live word make a difference in historical reality. . . . To do that requires that speech must not be conventional, reasonable, predictable; it must shock sensitivity, call attention to what is not noticed, break the routine, cause people to redescribe things that have long since seemed settled."[6] Jeremiah's words and images played upon the imagination of his community to convey God's new way.

Likewise, the language of Jesus was designed to shock its hearers into envisioning a different reality—the kingdom of God. According to biblical scholar Robert Tannehill, Jesus used "forceful and imaginative language," strong words, and vivid symbols in order to unseat the competing symbols and assumptions by which human beings structure their sinful lives.[7] Jesus created a new world by the power of his words; people entered into it and were changed. Jesus' words at the Last Supper were metaphor of the highest order: "This bread is my body broken for you." As Amos Wilder explained, "a true metaphor or symbol is more than a sign, it is a bearer of the reality to which it refers."[8]

Choose Specific Details That Show Credibility

When we use incarnational language in our preaching, it helps close the gap many of our listeners perceive between faith and "real life." More than 150 years ago, Ralph Waldo Emerson complained about a preacher who failed to connect with the lives of his listeners: "This man had ploughed and planted and talked and bought and sold; he had read books; he had eaten and drunken; his head aches, his heart throbs; he smiles and suffers; yet there was not a surmise, a hint, in all of the discourse, that he had ever lived at all."[9] As Fred Craddock explained, "When sermons are filled with expressions such as 'modern society,' 'scientists today,' 'today's youth,' 'global conflict,' 'many marriages,' or 'farm life in America,' no pulse races, no nerves twitch, no parishioner leans forward in rapt attention."[10] If a preacher says, "adolescents face many challenges," parishioners may nod politely while thinking "What do you know about it?" If the preacher says instead, "Fourteen-year-old Emily goes to Columbus Middle School. Four of her friends get drunk every month and three have confessed to cutting themselves," the congregation feels the preacher has credibility. Details demonstrate that the preacher knows what he or she is talking about.

Using simple, sensory language also allows our listeners to absorb the experience of the sermon along with us. For example, a preacher could simply say, "Moses was a stubborn and reluctant hero running from God." Statement of fact. However, if the preacher describes the catch in Moses' breath, the acrid smell of his sweat, the rough texture of the cloak in which he hid his face, as well as the implacable timbre in God's voice, listeners will experience Moses' resistance for themselves and make their own assessment of his character. Teachers of creative writing call this strategy "showing rather than telling." As Anton Chekhov said, "Don't tell me the moon is shining; show me the glint of light on broken glass."

Writing teacher Janet Burroway explained that all imaginative writing is made up of such concrete, significant details. "*Concrete* means that there is an image, something that can be seen, heard, smelled, tasted or touched. *Detail* means there is a degree of focus and specificity. *Significant* means that the specific image also suggests an abstraction, generalization, or judgment."[11] Detroit poet Elizabeth Volpe illustrated the use of concrete, significant details in her poem "Brewing in Eden":

> The Coffee Wars. The That-Milk-Is-Still-Perfectly-Good
> Wars. The Do-You-Really-Need-All-Those-Lights-On
> Wars. I scowl, and he growls. I notice he's chewing
> his corn flakes more noisily than usual, so I rattle the morning
> paper,
> as if shaking snakes from the newsprint. Then I inch the
> pages over
> until they are ever-so-slightly on top of his placemat,
> just barely touching his plate.[12]

"As if shaking snakes from the newsprint." The poem portrays a moment any couple would recognize. With its subtle humor and evocation of the fall, the images from this poem could be used in a wedding homily or a sermon on marriage.

Surprisingly, the more specific our word, the more universally it speaks. A few well-chosen details can represent a larger human experience. In the play *Death of a Salesman*, by Arthur Miller, the protagonist Willy Loman gave his mistress several pairs of new silk stockings, expensive and hard to acquire. In the next scene the audience saw Loman's wife mending a pair of her silk stockings at the kitchen table. Loman angrily told her to throw them out.[13] That particular detail—silk stockings—conveyed the universal human experience of guilt and betrayal.

Songwriter Ysaye Barnwell of Sweet Honey in the Rock invoked the principle of "the universal particular" to explain reactions to her song "No Mirrors." In the song, Barnwell described the unconditional love she received from her grandmother, something different from what she received from everyone else. "There were no mirrors in my nana's house," Barnwell sang. "So I never knew my skin was too black / I never knew my nose was too flat." She told an interviewer that people actually told her to pinch her nose every day to make it more pointy. "I could not be more specific about my own pain around how I look than to put into a song that my nose is broad, and I am black," she said. But when her group sang "No Mirrors," white women would cry in the front row, and white gay ensembles asked to sing the song. The details in the song about her skin and nose and ill-fitting clothes evoked for her listeners times in their own lives when they felt unlovely or unacceptable. "The more specific we can be, the more universal we are," Barnwell said. "It's a paradox—but it's true."[14] Specific details convey our shared humanity.

Express the Incarnation in Sensory Images

Preaching is a moment of incarnation. The expressive language of the sermon bears the reality of God's presence in a flesh-and-blood world. The preacher proclaims the Word made flesh to people who shovel snow, diaper babies, argue about money, steal the clicker, get lost in television, plot revenge, make love in passion or despair. Writer Reynolds Price challenged preachers not to flinch from embodiment of the Word: "The Old and New Testaments are unremittingly physical," Price said. "Failure to convey that reality is failure to tell the story, failure to confront and recreate the embarrassing and demanding corporeality of the original."[15] Though we preachers may be uneasy about our bodily selves, we are all "words made flesh," poet Franz Wright said. "A part of God is brought into physical reality in every human being, not just in Christ. Christ is the great sun that eclipses everyone else, but we all participate in some minute way."[16]

We may also shy away from sensory language because of our reading of the apostle Paul. Influenced by the dualism of Greek philosophy, we may assume that anything having to do with "flesh" is evil. However, Paul's understanding of "flesh" is more complex than first appears, as biblical scholar Leander Keck has said. For Paul, "flesh (*sarx*) is not identical with *soma*, body, nor is it the substance of the body. Rather, like Spirit, flesh is a domain of power, a sphere of influence in which one lives." Though Paul does pit flesh and Spirit against each other sometimes, "he does not equate flesh and sin," Keck said. "The struggle between Spirit and flesh is not a battle between higher and lower nature, between our bodily drives and our minds or spirits. Rather the struggle is between the power of the eschatological future and the power of the empirical present."[17] Paul did not reject or condemn our physical bodies; rather, he believed they are "members" of Christ. "Glorify God in your body," Paul said (1 Cor. 6:20).

Understanding preaching as part of the incarnation, we ask ourselves, "What specific image or sensory event expresses the truth I have experienced?" Barbara Brown Taylor demonstrated the use of sensory language in her description of how members of the early church fell away from the initial passion of their faith: "Little by little, Christians became devoted to their comforts instead: the soft couch, the flannel sheets, the leg of lamb roasted with rosemary."[18] (Notice how the mixing of modern and ancient images implicates her own hearers as well.) Taylor demonstrated the cumulative power of sensory language in a series of examples on the difference between having the right answer and doing the right thing: "A right answer has never picked up a frightened child, or put an ice chip in the mouth of a dying friend. A right answer has never written a check to the Red Cross, or pried up stinking linoleum from a kitchen floor in the ninth ward of New Orleans."[19]

Prefer the Words of Ordinary Speech

Incarnational language uses ordinary speech—simple words, concrete images, specific details. Wherever you can, substitute concrete for abstract, specific for general, common for academic. For example, instead of saying, "A period of unfavorable weather set in," say, "It rained every day for a week." Or, instead of "He showed satisfaction as he took possession of his well-earned reward," write "He grinned as he pocketed the coin." These examples come from a slim, classic text on good writing, *The Elements of Style*, by William Strunk Jr. and E. B. White, a book worth reviewing once a year.[20] What we need to say can usually be expressed with common words, speechwriter Peggy Noonan explained: "Most of the important things you will ever say or hear in your life are composed of simple, good, sturdy words. 'I love you.' 'It's over.' 'It's a boy.' 'We're going to win.' 'He's dead.' . . . Simple words . . . are like pickets in a fence, slim and unimpressive on their own but sturdy and effective when strung together."[21] Drawn from the vocabulary of ordinary life, incarnational language relies mostly on simple words, believing they will be equal to the task.

Beware of clunky, managerial phrases that move like sludge. Kathleen Norris described a prayer she heard that went something like this: "Our communication with Jesus tends to be too infrequent to experience the transformation in our lives that you want us to have." Oh, dear. "It seemed less a prayer than a memo from one professional to another," Norris said.[22] How much more powerful that prayer would have been if it had said simply, "We don't talk to you often enough, Jesus. How, then, will you be able to change us?"

Does this mean that we can never use abstract language or theological terms? No. Occasionally we will want to use one of our million-dollar seminary words like eschatology or ecclesiology. Sometimes a large or unusual word is the only one that will do. We earn the right to use abstract words, however, by surrounding them with words that refer to real things. We situate abstract ideas in a mass of matter, like flecks of shiny mica in a chunk of gneiss. What Ezra Pound said of poetry applies to sermons as well: "To use the language of common speech, but to employ always the exact word, not the nearly-exact, not the merely decorative word. . . . Poetry should render particulars exactly and not deal in vague generalities, however magnificent and sonorous."[23]

Don't Explain the Metaphor

We can trust language to do its own work. When I asked him what advice he would give preachers, poet Thomas Lynch said, "Don't explain the metaphor, just give it." If our hearers don't understand the metaphor right away, so much the better. They will mull it over during the week. The tension created by the different elements of the metaphor will draw them deeper into its reality. I once used portions of Tim Gautreaux's short story "Welding with Children" in a sermon on sacrificial commitment, ending the sermon with the metaphor that Gautreaux used to close the story. Bruton, the main character, is playing with his grandsons, Freddie and Nu-Nu, in his newly cleaned back yard:

> "We gonna put a tire swing on that tall willow oak there, first off," [Bruton says].
>
> "All right. Can you cut a drain hole in the bottom so the rainwater won't stay in it?" [Freddie] . . . puts a hand on top of the baby's head.
>
> "Yep."
>
> "A big steel-belt tire?"
>
> "Sounds like a plan. . . ." Nu-Nu looked at me and yelled, "Da-da." . . . I put him on my knee, facing away toward the cool green branches of my biggest willow oak.
>
> "Even Nu-Nu can ride the tire," Freddie said.
>
> "He can fit the circle in the middle," I told him.[24]

A parishioner approached me at choir practice on Thursday night saying she'd been thinking about the sermon all week. She asked what the final image meant. I asked her, "What do you think?"

"I think the tire swing is like the love of God—we're held in the center of it," she said.

I didn't have to explain the metaphor. She got it.

Try This

• One exercise that helps us create incarnational language is "sensory exploration." In this exercise we pay attention to the Scripture through our senses, looking for concrete images and details evoked by the text or its context. If we were to go through Exodus 14 with our senses, for example, the exercise might go like this:

a) Go through the text with your nose. Do you smell anything? It may be the dank, fishy smell of shallow water, or the musk of unwashed bodies.

b) Go through the text with your body: Do you feel anything? Hot sun through the robe on your back. The heaviness of shoulders and legs that have walked far with heavy burdens. Assume the posture of the characters in the text—how does it feel?

c) Go through the text with your ears: Do you hear anything? Seagulls crying as they wheel above your head. Reeds rustling in a strong wind. Small children whimpering with fear and fatigue. The far-off rumble of chariots.

d) Go through the text with your eyes: Do you see anything? A cloud of dust on the horizon raised by the feet of the Egyptian soldiers. The dark pillar in front of Moses.

e) Do you taste anything? You taste bile in your mouth because you are afraid.

Taste. Touch. Smell. Sight. Hearing. Five ways for the Scripture to come alive for us and our people.

Now try the exercise with Mark 14:66–72, Peter's denial of Jesus.

Substitute Vivid Language for Clichés

Watch, then, for vivid language. Alert yourself to colorful phrases, simile, metaphor, personification, and so on wherever they occur. Figures of speech will crop up in deliciously unexpected places, from the lips of teenagers, small children, comedians, and old guys at family reunions. Comedian Jeff Foxworthy is particularly good at simile. I heard him say something like this in a "Redneck" comedy sketch: "If your butt looks like two raccoons rassling in a fifty-pound feed sack, say 'No' to spandex." Practice substituting something surprising or apt for clichés. Janet Burroway suggested that we use creative-writing techniques such as brainstorming and free association to create fresh language. "The less you clamp down on your dreaming, the less you concede to logic, the less you allow your internal critic to shut you up, the more likely you are to produce the startling-dead-on comparison," Burroway said. "Cut logic loose, focus on what you see, taste, touch. Free-write, and let the strangeness in you surface."[25]

Burroway's advice may be hard for us preachers to follow because we spend so much of our public life being proper, polite, correct, and careful. But in the privacy of our studies, who will see? We don't have to use everything we imagine in our sermons. We are free to experiment, practice, adapt, revise, like Jesus, who looked around and said, "Consider the lilies of the field," or "You are the salt of the earth."

Avoid Purple Prose

Once we get excited about vivid language, however, we may get carried away with it. Veteran preachers caution against over description. "I'm not looking for sentences like, 'The sun rose slowly in a dusky haze over the pink hills of Judea,'" Hulitt Gloer told a group of preachers at Calvin College.[26] Fred Craddock agreed: "Narration and description are with emotional restraint and economy of words. . . . Too many adjectives in effect tell the listeners what to see and hear and how they are to respond to what is described."[27] The following sentence by Scott Palmer of Oregon demonstrates how *not* to handle description. Palmer's sentence won second place in a contest in "purple prose" held by the English department of San Jose State University in 2007. The challenge: to compose the worst opening sentence. "The Barents sea heaved and churned like a tortured animal in pain, the howling wind tearing packets of icy green water from the shuddering crests of the waves, atomizing it into mist that was again laid flat by the growing fury of the storm as Kevin Tucker switched off the bedside light in his Tuba City, Arizona, single-wide trailer and by the time the phone woke him at 7:38, had pretty much blown itself out with no damage."[28] You get the idea of what to avoid. Include only those details that are necessary to make your point.

Well-written sermons take time and work. "Most of the great preachers have been word artists," James Earl Massey said.[29] The incarnate word is a *deliberate* word, chosen, weighed, sweated over. Here is the anguish of revising whole paragraphs, or even starting over. Barbara Brown Taylor told how she "auditions" the words in her sermons: "The page is the stage where the words audition and rehearse. They file in to show me what they can do. I weed them out. They explain themselves to me. I ask for more feeling."[30] To put ourselves in obedience to the exact word or the clearest image is a spiritual discipline as demanding as prayer or fasting. It challenges our laziness. It goes against our instincts. We won't always do it. But when we do, when the words sing together like music, it is worth every drop of sweat.

Try This

• The following writing exercise, called "clustering," was developed by writing teacher Gabriele Rico. It's based on brain research that suggests that human beings have two ways of knowing. Left-brain, what Rico calls "Sign mind," is "largely occupied with rational, logical presentations of reality"—analyzing, defining, specifying. Words are used as signs to denote a narrow and specific meaning. Right-brain, or "Design mind," perceives reality in complex images and organic patterns, using language to evoke a cluster of meanings and feeling. Thoughts and images often come in clusters like grapes. Both sides of the brain, both ways of knowing, are crucial for clear and powerful communication, Rico said. However, since the Sign mind can overpower the Design mind early in the writing process, we need exercises to free and cultivate right-brain capabilities, particularly when we are generating ideas.[31] This is Rico's method:

a) Choose a nucleus word, phrase, or impression. (e.g., JOYOUS or AFRAID)
b) Write the word or phrase in a circle, leaving room around it on the page.
c) "What comes to mind when you think of the word? . . . Let words or phrases radiate outward from the nucleus, and draw a circle around each of them. Connect those associations that seem related with lines." Write as rapidly as you can, with a relaxed receptivity.
d) If nothing comes, doodle by putting in arrows or darkening the lines of what you have written already. Your Sign

mind may try to interfere or take over. "Should you experience resistance to the novelty of clustering, go through the motions of drawing circles and lines around a stimulus word. . . . Simply relax and doodle, letting the circles and lines shape a pleasing pattern." You may find yourself filling in those "inviting empty circles" with associations to the nucleus word.

e) Stop clustering when you have a sense of "Ah, that's what I meant," or "Aha, that's what I want to write about."

f) Begin writing sentences about your chosen word, writing for eight to ten minutes. "Your aim is to produce a self-contained vignette" on the word you have chosen.[32]

Below is an example of a cluster and free-writing I did on the word *otter*.

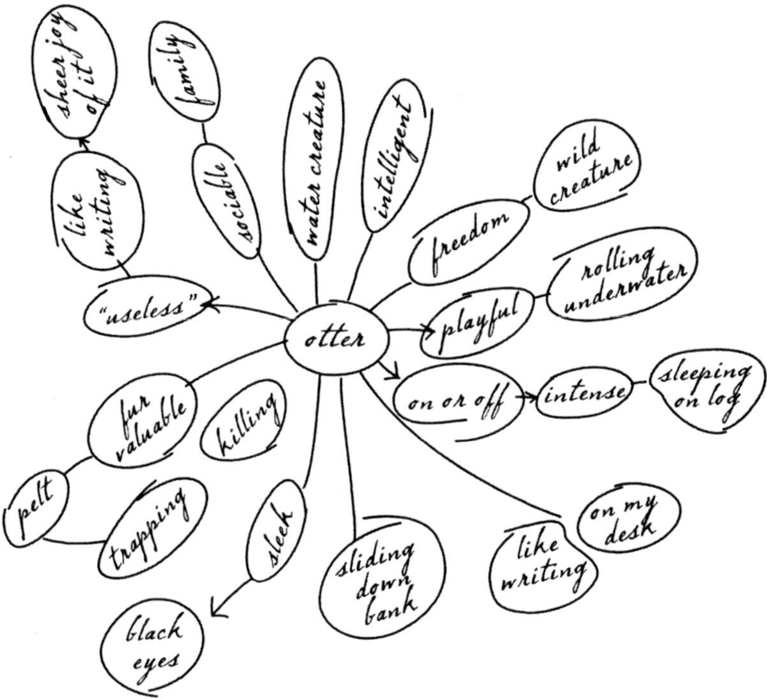

Figure 5.1. Free-writing on "otter"

The otter on my desk, a detailed statue two and a half inches high, represents the playfulness and freedom I rarely feel. Recalling the river otters I saw turning somersaults under our canoe at Oxbow Bend, I long for the rare visit of a playful urge. I remember how keenly I scanned the tannin-dark waters of the Tahquamenon River for an otter on our last trip north.

Winter sadness presses in on me, threatening to stall my fingers, urging me toward self-defeat. The statue is an ineffectual totem against all that, unless . . . by some grace of imagination I can live back into the sleek, wet, thick-furred intelligence that slides quickly through cold dark waters and finds some ice-covered bank down which to slide. Webbed feet push against water and bubbles rise to the surface, soon to be followed by bright, feral eyes. This otter is heedless of the scientist's insistence upon measured, useful life or the trapper's greedy tally of the value of its pelt. Only this: the black tangles of tree roots and hollowed rooms of riverbed flash by its protected, observing eye, and the great gray sky above the water is simply the lighter element in which to swim.

• Compare versions of some of your favorite passages in the Bible. Consult the *Tanakh* (The Jewish Bible) for Hebrew texts and include a paraphrase such as Eugene Peterson's *The Message*. Which versions have more evocative power? Why? Note where translators have heightened or blunted vivid language.

For Further Study

Annie Dillard. *Teaching a Stone to Talk: Expeditions and Encounters*. New York: HarperCollins, 1982.

Chapter Six

Time to Revise

Avoid Last-Minute Stress

It was 10:30 p.m. and the raucous laughter of *Saturday Night Live* was coming from our living room. I'd done it to myself again. Coffee cooling in my cup, Bible and commentaries beside me, computer screen glowing a pale green, my sermon wasn't done. Not anywhere close. I heard my husband laughing at a skit. Soon he would be poking his head in my study to ask, "Sermon done yet?" and would trudge off to bed alone.

We all have those weeks when an unexpected pileup of funerals, hospital calls, office crises, sickness, denominational responsibilities, or family issues delays our sermon preparation to the last minute. Life happens. I know at least two colleagues, however, for whom Saturday night sermons are the rule rather than the exception. One, a perfectionist, puts off sermon writing because that is the only way she can circumvent the fear that it won't be good enough. The other prefers a loose, stream-of-consciousness style that Saturday-night preparation facilitates. "I work best under pressure," he says. There's only one problem. When we leave our preparation to the last minute, we deprive ourselves of one of the most effective sermon techniques available: revision.

Revision may be a dirty word to some, conjuring up painful memories of school papers scrawled with a teacher's angry red script: "awk" (awkward), "agr" (verb agreement), "run-on" (run-on sentence), "DO OVER!" Not wanting to recall schoolroom shaming, we leave our preparation to the last minute so the Critic can stay safely asleep. But after twenty-five years of writing sermons, I know this: revision works.

Revision clarifies thought, helps us remove unnecessary material, and allows us to replace a so-so illustration with one that is just right. Revision anticipates where listeners might have difficulty. Is this transition clear? Is this application relevant? Those of us who preach more than once a Sunday often find that the last version of the sermon is better than the first because we continue to revise instinctively while we preach. A quizzical or offended look on a listener's face will send us back to our office between services, hastily scribbling a change in the margin, or making adjustments on the fly. Revising ahead of time increases our confidence in our material, allowing us to relax a little more when the moment arrives. Revision works.

I recall an Advent sermon written under the press of holiday gatherings. When we left on Saturday night for a family dinner, I had what I considered a decent draft: preachable, but I wasn't happy with it. During the ride home, it became clear to me that the order of the middle paragraphs was scrambled. I pulled it out again before going to bed and rearranged it. The flow of ideas was much clearer, and the changed order helped me focus the ending more emphatically. I got a note from a parishioner later in the week that read, "I especially enjoyed your sermon with the chainsaw sound effects. Even my pokey old husband liked it. Coming from him, that is a real compliment." The right ideas were all there, but had I not gone through the final revision, I doubt the sermon would have had the same impact.

When it comes to revision, there are two issues: giving ourselves enough time to work and knowing what to change.

Protect Time to Prepare

Some of the best preachers allocate eight or more hours a week to sermon preparation. Harry Emerson Fosdick said that preachers should spend one hour in the study for every minute in the pulpit. Most of us don't have that luxury. However, managing our schedules allows us to protect the time we need for sermon preparation. It is important not to let other responsibilities consistently erode our preaching work. When are you at your best, your most creative and energetic? When during the day does your energy flag and your brain get fuzzy? Reserve some of your "prime time" for writing the first draft of the sermon. Know your own rhythms, then protect your sermon time as carefully as you would a counseling session or a meeting with the church council. The advice Dorothea Brande gave to aspiring writers applies to preachers as well:

> Teach yourself to write at a given moment [say four o'clock]. . . . Now this is very important, and can hardly be emphasized too strongly: *you have decided to write at four o'clock, and at four o'clock write you must! No excuses can be given.* If at four o'clock you find yourself deep in conversation, you must excuse yourself and keep your engagement. Your agreement is a debt of honor, and must be scrupulously observed. . . . However halting or perfunctory the writing is, *write*. . . . You must learn to disregard every loophole the wily unconscious points out to you. If you consistently, doggedly, refuse to be beguiled, you will have your reward. The unconscious will suddenly give in charmingly, and begin to write gracefully and well.[1]

Protecting time for sermon preparation gives us the freedom to enter the messy stage of sermon writing, that frustrating and crucial phase when we spin out ideas, follow interesting paths, tease out associations, raise deep questions. "Allow yourself to be in the muddle, to get everything out that occurs to you, because the new lead may be where the piece really needs to go," poetry teacher Mary Jo Firth-Gillett told our workshop.[2] The same advice holds for sermons. I've found that I can approach sermon preparation with less urgency and less control. Urgency makes me settle too quickly into predetermined conclusions. My desire for control of the process often inhibits the leading of the Holy Spirit.

Break It into Small Tasks

Another time management technique that can benefit preachers is to break a large task into small parts. Anne Lamott illustrated this strategy in her writing guide, *Bird by Bird:*

> Thirty years ago my older brother, who was ten years old at the time, was trying to get a report on birds written that he'd had three months to write, which was due the next day. We were out at our family cabin in Bolinas, and he was at the kitchen table close to tears, surrounded by binder paper and pencils and unopened books on birds, immobilized by the hugeness of the task ahead. Then my father sat down beside him, put his arm around my brother's shoulder, and said, "Bird by bird, buddy. Just take it bird by bird."[3]

When we break the large task of completing a sermon into smaller parts, we can make use of small units of time. In half an hour before a meeting, we can check a biblical reference, do a word study, or search for a specific illustration in our files or on the Internet. We can do exegetical study one day, read supporting historical, theological, or pastoral material on another.

Planning ahead also helps with time management. Whether or not we use the lectionary, we can choose and review texts for the next three or six months. I have found that material begins to cluster around the texts like steel shavings around a magnet. One spring the evangelism committee of our church planned a "Bring a Friend Sunday" for the approaching September, asking me to preach on the Great Commission from Matthew 28:16–20. While reading a denominational magazine over the summer, I came across a story about a thirty-one-year-old Haitian preacher who brought more than one hundred persons to Christ. The story about him went into the file.

Observe Sabbath to Refresh Your Spirit

Time management and spiritual vitality are closely related. Our sermons may be dull and plodding because we ourselves are exhausted and depleted. Late in his life, John Wesley admonished one of his preachers about the importance of providing oneself with spiritual nourishment in the form of daily reading and prayer:

> O begin! Fix some part of every day for private exercises. You may acquire the taste which you have not; what is tedious at first will afterwards be pleasant. Whether you like it or no, read and pray daily. It is for your life; there is no other way: else you will be a trifler all your days, and a pretty superficial preacher. Do justice to your own soul; give it time and means to grow. Do not starve yourself any longer.[4]

Set aside time to pray daily and practice different forms of prayer. Our spiritual disciplines may need to include fasting from certain kinds of food in order to be our most alert and creative.

Also, protect time to rest and play. Because we work on Sunday, we preachers do not get to observe Sabbath in the same way as our parishioners. I've found that it is vital for my own health and creativity to take a whole day off once a week. On this day I am "off duty." I don't have to produce anything. I am free to enjoy my family and friends and the beauty of the earth. After I am rested, I often get new ideas for sermon planning, and am able to see where a specific sermon needs to be revised. United Methodist Bishop Linda Lee felt so strongly about the observance of Sabbath that she mandated a retreat on the subject for the seven hundred active pastors in her area. "In our passionate rush to be helpful, we miss something sacred when we fail to observe Sabbath," she said.[5] The retreat leader, Wayne Muller, agreed: "Weariness can be a bushel that hides our light," he said. "In med school, when I was learning to be exhausted, I was hoping that the numbers would tell me what my heart couldn't hear. When I took time to rest and pray, my wisdom returned. If we do not rest, we will do good badly."[6]

The day we choose to observe our Sabbath will depend upon our church and family schedules. It is a challenge to coordinate time for relaxation with family and friends when their free time often coincides with the busiest part of our schedule (evenings and weekends). But it can be done. The flexibility of the pastoral schedule also allows us to take "little Sabbaths" throughout the week—a walk in the sunshine in the early afternoon, a quiet hour with a good book, lunch with a friend. Such moments are like sips of cold water on a hot day, refreshing body and spirit. No matter how carefully we manage our time, however, we finally have to let go and let God. There is an infinite horizon of sermon preparation, parish responsibilities, and family needs. We give our work to God and trust that God will bless it. Not everything depends on us, after all. God was and is and will be at work in the world through the endless creativity of the Holy Spirit. Hallelujah!

Use Tricks to Overcome Writing Resistance

When we have faithfully protected our time to write our sermons, we may sit down and find that we are resisting the actual writing. I remember a seminary classmate who had his study in the basement next to his workshop. His wife came down one evening and found him turning a table leg on his lathe. "I thought you told me you were writing your sermon!" she said. Become aware of your own patterns of resistance. Use tricks and bribes if you have to. When I am avoiding a sermon, I tell myself, "You can have chocolate or coffee if you just sit down." Or, "You only have to sit down for fifty minutes." I set a battery-powered kitchen timer for fifty minutes. Often, by the time fifty minutes have elapsed, ideas have begun to flow and the momentum of the developing sermon begins to carry me along. When the timer goes off, I get up, stretch, refill my coffee cup, whatever. Brief breaks keep us fresh. Moving about helps ease the strain in shoulders hunched too long over the computer. Then it is time to set the timer again.

As the monastics did, you may also find it helpful to intersperse mental work with physical labor. Any repetitive, manual task—weeding a garden, mowing a lawn, peeling vegetables, folding clothes, sweeping a floor—can free the mind and prompt insight. Doing some gentle stretches or taking a walk may also get your brain juices flowing again. When you round the corner to your house or church, the thought that has been eluding you may present itself in your brain. (Where have you been? What took you so long?)

If these tricks don't work, try one or more of these exercises adapted from teacher Janet Burroway's instruction to help writers who are stuck:

Try This

• Rewrite the theme of your sermon in the form of one of the following: an instruction pamphlet; a letter to the complaints department; directions for a skit; a television commercial; a love song.

• Take a paragraph you like and highlight a word that strikes you, that seems to capture the spirit of the paragraph or sermon. Cluster the word, free-write for ten minutes, and see what emerges.

• Read over the last paragraph where you got stuck, then put it aside. Begin writing fast and loosely, starting every thought with "it's like . . . it's like . . . it's like . . ." One thought might be a memory that could be worked into a story. Another thought might relate to a different Scripture passage that counters or supports your text. A strong feeling might emerge, or a physical sensation. See if any of these offer you a way back into the sermon.[7]

Deal with Sermon Block

If you get stuck deeply, however, week after week, you may have sermon block. This was a significant problem for me several years into my ministry. I recall some terrible Saturday nights when I read novels instead of writing, getting too little sleep, irritating my husband and disappointing my congregation. Part of my problem in those years was self-care. I had personal issues that were interfering with my ability to preach. It was like trying to write with someone knocking on the wall in the next room. With the help of good friends and a trustworthy counselor, I was able to resolve my own issues enough to focus on what God wanted to say through the Scripture to my congregation.

Sermon block may manifest itself in several ways. We may avoid direct engagement with the text or the people. (Been there, done that.) We may panic and pull the scholars from the shelves, hiding behind their interpretations instead of pushing through to our own. (Been there, done that.) Or, we may compose a lecture on the ideas in the Scripture, safe in the comfortable abstractions of academic language. (Been there, done that.) O pity us poor preachers! It's no wonder our sermons stumble sometimes. We are hurried, harried, overworked, afraid.

If someone we love disapproves of our being a preacher, or has extremely high expectations of us, it may be fear that blocks our sermon writing. We may be afraid of failing. Or, conversely, we may be afraid of succeeding. Sometimes our need to write a great sermon can interfere with writing any sermon at all. Eugene Lowry confessed that "there is a kind of sermonic drought that is apt to set in upon me whenever I am intentionally working on a sermon."[8] Frozen in fear, we may call ourselves lazy, procrastinators, failures. However, the best cure for fear is love, as 1 John 4:18 says: "Perfect love casts out fear." God loves us. God loves our people. Enthusiasm, more than self-discipline, is what sustains us over the long haul, for the root meaning of "enthusiasm" is *entheos*—God in us.

So, let us be gentle with ourselves. Take the next small step. Give yourself permission to write a rotten first draft, trusting that God will give you the next draft, and the next. We are learning how to write sermons over weeks, months, years, a lifetime. We will get better. And God will take whatever we offer, and use it in ways we can only faintly imagine.

Say It Out Loud

This being said, we still can do what is in our power. How to revise for greatest effect? First, read what you have written aloud. This is standard advice for creative-writing students. If true for writers, whose words stand on the page and can be returned to by the reader, how much more true for speakers, whose listeners have only one shot at understanding. Speechwriter Peggy Noonan underscored this advice in her book *Simply Speaking*: "You must be able to say the sentences you write. Once you've finished a first draft . . . stand up and read it aloud. *Where you falter, alter*. . . . Sentences must be short and sayable not only for you but for your listeners. They're trying to absorb what you say, and if your sentences are too dense with information they won't be able to follow." Noonan held up professional newswriters for network anchors as an example. "They write for listeners as opposed to readers. Sometimes when they are tired and the day goes long, TV writers see themselves as convicts on chain gangs with sledgehammers, 'breakin' big ones into little ones.'"[9] Barbara Brown Taylor also emphasized that preachers are writing not for the page, but for the ear:

> What's lovely on the page is often too heavy for the air. Now that's only logical, if you think about it, because a page is so much more substantial than air. A page can hold hundreds of words together, tethered to one another by commas and semicolons, so that a reader can go back and make sure that none have gotten away. . . . The words will still be there waiting for you on the page, as patient as rabbits in the pen. But none of that works in the air. In order to survive that medium, words have to be fast and light. Pack too many syllables in them and they will sink before they have gone three feet out of your mouth. If you link a long string of them together with a semicolon in the middle, then you can watch half of them take a wrong turn because those in back lost track of those in front.[10]

Can you speak it easily? If you can't say it easily, they won't hear it easily. Rewrite.

Trim Everything That Doesn't Advance the Theme

Second, keep the theme, or focus, or aim of your sermon in front of you. Ask yourself: Is my theme substantive? Relevant? Does all of the material relate tightly to my theme? Am I trying to do too much? A perennial problem of preachers is that we try to preach two or three sermons at one time. Writer Tim Gautreaux compared narrative structure to a machine that has no extraneous parts. "If you buy a new car, go out in the driveway and open the hood, do you see a spark plug scotch-taped to the side of the block with a note on it, 'Found this on the factory floor. Thought you might like to have it'? No, everything under the hood has a purpose. . . . Everything is doing something. . . . Sometimes the quality of a story depends upon not what's there but what's been left out."[11] Remove any elements of the sermon that do not advance your theme. Purpose drives form.

Review Parts for Effective Order

Third, review the order of the elements of the sermon. Structural issues can weaken the best sermons. Do the ideas flow in logical or organic order? If you are unsure, rearrange them and see. Also, look carefully at transitions from one portion of the sermon to the next. Do the transitions establish clear relationship between the different parts of the sermon? Can your listeners follow you? Some examples of transitional words or phrases are "yet," "however," "for example," "on another occasion," "therefore."

A sermon that proceeds as a series of images will not have the same kind of transitions as a carefully reasoned argument. In an image sermon, the transitions may be sensory rather than logical. Every time you change scenes you need to locate your hearers immediately in time and space. You can do so by describing a person, a setting, an object, or a sensation. (Review the three scenes in the example of the refrain sermon in chap. 3 to see how sensory details help establish a scene.) You may set up a framework ahead of time to identify images. In a wedding homily shaped for the mass-media generation, Thomas Troeger imagined a series of photos taken on a couple's first, fifth, tenth, and fiftieth wedding anniversaries. The progress of the years and different phrases in the wedding vows provided the framework for the sermon.[12] A change in vocal quality or a long pause can also alert your hearers that you are switching scenes.

Look at Line by Line

The final task of revision is to review the smaller units of the sermon, the paragraphs and sentences. Wherever you can, replace general words with specific ones, weak verbs with stronger ones, passive verbs with active ones. Choose words with pictures in them.

General: They helped restore property damaged by Hurricane Katrina.

Specific: They bagged debris from a flooded clinic in St. Bernard Parish: magazines, patient records, medical reference books, soggy rolls of gauze, and the occasional syringe.

Weak: He put the book on the table.

Stronger: He slammed the book on the table.

Weak: He corrected her statement.

Stronger: "You're wrong," he said.

Passive: My first visit to the Holy Land will always be remembered by me.

Active: I will always remember my first visit to the Holy Land.

Passive: There were a great number of dry bones lying in the valley.

Active: Dry bones covered the valley floor.

Try This

Pick a random paragraph from a sermon you preached recently. Check for places where you can cut weak words and substitute stronger ones, changing passive verbs to active ones and cutting unnecessary words. Brevity communicates vigor.

What Language Shall I Borrow?

Revision takes time and effort, but every minute we spend in revision makes our sermons stronger. "Good writing is ten percent inspiration—ninety percent perspiration." Though it is tempting to preserve what feels like the freshness of our first creation, and once in a while, a seemingly perfect sermon does come to us whole, as a gift, most sermons can be improved by revision. There's no way around it. "Writing *is* revision," poet Jeffrey Skinner said.[13]

However much we tinker with structure or diddle with word choice, though, at some point, language itself breaks down. We cannot adequately express the awe, wonder, and gratitude we feel at God's love and grace. "What language shall I borrow, to thank thee, dearest friend?"[14] Even our best work is a pale evocation. Ah, well. Once I watched two Tibetan monks construct a sand mandala as a temporary exhibit in an art museum. Draped in orange robes, the monks knelt beside a low table, tapping brilliantly colored grains of sand from metal funnels onto a surface of black slate. They shaped white, blue, black, red, yellow, and green grains into intricate geometric patterns. The display notes said it would take them three to five days to complete the design. The notes also said that the monks would sweep away the whole marvelous creation after it was finished. I watched for a long time, enchanted. The careful, attentive rhythm of their movements was like a dance.

In similar fashion, we preachers work attentively within a long tradition, crafting as carefully as we can a thing of beauty, delighting in the play of detail and form. Though the intervening week will sweep away our creation, the rhythm of prayer, study, writing, revision, and delivery is our own dance. Though our words will dissipate in the air, we are given the grace to begin and begin again. To God be the glory.

Notes

Introduction

1. Fred B. Craddock, *Overhearing the Gospel* (Nashville: Abingdon Press, 1978), 13.
2. Ibid., *Preaching* (Nashville: Abingdon Press, 1985), 79.
3. Terence E. Fretheim, *The Book of Genesis: Introduction, Commentary, and Reflections*, in *The New Interpreter's Bible: A Commentary in Twelve Volumes*, vol. 1 (Nashville: Abingdon Press, 1994), 343.
4. Michael Card, *Scribbling in the Sand* (Downers Grove, IL: InterVarsity Press, 2004), http.www.ivpress.com/spotlight/2317.php.
5. John Ciardi and Miller Williams, *How Does a Poem Mean?* 2nd ed. (Boston: Houghton Mifflin Co., 1975), xix–xx.
6. Eugene L. Lowry, *The Homiletical Plot: The Sermon as Narrative Art Form*, expanded ed. (Louisville, KY: Westminster John Knox Press, 2001), 103–4.
7. *Chariots of Fire*, videocassette, directed by Hugh Hudson (1981; Warner Home Video, 2000).

Chapter One: Use a Hook

1. "Never hire a ferret to do a weasel's job," Budweiser commercial, Super Bowl, 1998.
2. Betty White, "Candler Professor Practices What He Teaches," *Atlanta Journal*, May 30, 1987, 1–B.
3. Barnaby Conrad, *The Complete Guide to Writing Fiction* (Cincinnati, OH: Writer's Digest Books, 1990), 15–16.
4. Janet Burroway, *Imaginative Writing: The Elements of Craft* (New York: Addison, Wesley Longman, 2003), 181.

5. Eugene L. Lowry, *How to Preach a Parable: Designs for Narrative Sermons* (Nashville: Abingdon Press, 1989), 32–33.
6. Ibid., *The Homiletical Plot: The Sermon as Narrative Art Form* (Atlanta: John Knox Press, 1980), 23.
7. Lowry, *Parable*, 33.
8. Barbara Brown Taylor, "Life Giving Fear," in *Home by Another Way* (Boston: Cowley Publications, 1999), 69.
9. Charles Dickens, *A Tale of Two Cities* (New York: Random House, 1996), 3.
10. Frederick Buechner, "The Power of God and the Power of Man," *The Magnificent Defeat* (San Francisco: Harper & Row, 1966), 28.
11. James M. Cain, *The Postman Always Rings Twice* (New York: Grossett & Dunlap, 1934), 3.
12. Susan Howatch, *Mystical Paths* (New York: Alfred A. Knopf, 1992), 3.
13. Sondra Willobee, "Limping but Blessed" (sermon, First United Methodist Church, Farmington, MI, August 4, 2002).
14. Opening scene, *Tender Mercies*, videocassette, dir. Bruce Beresford (1983; Burbank, CA: Warner Home Video, 2002).
15. Charles Dickens, *A Christmas Carol and Other Stories* (Pleasantville, NY: Reader's Digest, 1988), 15.
16. Thomas Troeger, *Creating Fresh Images for Preaching* (Valley Forge, PA: Judson Press, 1982), 52.
17. Edgar Allan Poe, "The Tell-Tale Heart," in *Oxford Book of American Short Stories*, ed. Joyce Carol Oates (New York: Oxford University Press, 1992), 92.
18. Jung Young Lee, "The New Family in Christ," *Sermons to the Twelve* (Nashville: Abingdon Press, 1988), 85.
19. Benjamin E. Mays, "Thanksgiving," in *Outstanding Black Sermons, Volume 3*, ed. Milton E. Owens Jr. (Valley Forge, PA: Judson Press, 1982), 47.
20. F. Scott Fitzgerald, *The Great Gatsby* (New York: Charles Scribner's Sons, 1925, 2004), 2.
21. Barbara Brown Taylor, "Out of the Whirlwind," in *Home By Another Way*, 162.
22. Leo Tolstoy, *Anna Karenina*, trans. Richard Pevear and Larissa Volokhonsky (New York: Penguin Putnam, 2000), 1.
23. Barbara Brown Taylor, "Show Me a Sign," in *Home by Another Way*, 47.
24. Howard Thurman, "Patriotism Quotes," from Wisdom Quotes: Quotations to Inspire and Challenge, Jone Johnson Lewis, www.wisdomquotes.com.
25. Oscar Wilde, *Oscar Wilde's Wit and Wisdom: A Book of Quotations* (Mineola, NY: Dover Publications, 1998), 50.
26. Edmund A. Steimle, "The Eye of the Storm," reprinted in *Preaching the Story*, by Edmund A. Steimle, Morris J. Niedenthal, Charles L. Rice (Philadelphia: Fortress Press, 1980), 122.
27. Sondra Willobee, "United We Stand" (sermon, First United Methodist Church, Farmington, MI, June 20, 2004).

28. Thomas Lynch, "A Conversation with James VandenBosch" (lecture, Festival of Faith and Writing, Calvin College, Grand Rapids, MI, April 24, 2004, and Bear River Writers' Conference, Walloon Lake, Petoskey, MI, June 1, 2002).
29. Fred B. Craddock, *Preaching* (Nashville: Abingdon Press, 1985), 167.
30. Douglas E. Nelson, "Raging Faith," in *A Chorus of Witnesses*, ed. Thomas G. Long and Cornelius Plantinga Jr. (Grand Rapids: Eerdmans, 1994), 44.
31. Elizabeth Achtemeier, "Of Children and Streets and the Kingdom," in Long and Plantinga, *Chorus of Witnesses*, 63.
32. Fred B. Craddock, "Praying through Clenched Teeth," in *How to Preach a Parable: Designs for Narrative Sermon*, by Eugene L. Lowry (Nashville: Abingdon Press, 1989), 142.
33. Dennis M. Willis, "Noah Was a Good Man," in Lowry, *How to Preach a Parable*, 42.
34. L. Susan Bond, "Coming Home," in *Patterns of Preaching*, ed. Ronald J. Allen (St. Louis: Chalice Press, 1998), 65.
35. Barbara Brown Taylor, "The Yes and No Brothers," in *Home by Another Way*, 187.

Chapter Two: Inspired Imagination

1. Paul Scott Wilson, *The Imagination of the Heart* (Nashville: Abingdon Press, 1988), 20.
2. Bill Wylie-Kellermann, e-mail message to friends, July 2, 2005.
3. Fred B. Craddock, *Preaching* (Nashville: Abingdon Press, 1985), 86.
4. Thomas Troeger, *Imagining a Sermon* (Nashville: Abingdon Press, 1990), 106.
5. Harold Fickett, "A Vocation of Fiction" (Spanning the Gap: The Artist's Calling, a Writing and Arts Festival, sponsored by the Milton Center, Kansas Newman College, and *Image: A Journal of the Arts and Religion*, Wichita, KS, November 12, 1994).
6. Russell Baker, *Growing Up* (New York: Congdon & Weed, 1982), 9–10. I used this excerpt from Baker in a sermon for Pentecost Sunday titled "Seeing Visions and Dreaming Dreams."
7. Bonnie Friedman, "Message from a Cloud of Flies: On Distraction," *Writing Past Dark* (New York: Harper Collins, 1993), quoted in Janet Burroway, *Writing Fiction* (New York: Harper Collins, 1996), 16–19.
8. Craddock, *Preaching*, 135–36.
9. D. H. Lawrence, "The Song of a Man Who Has Come Through," *The Norton Anthology of Modern Poetry*, ed. Richard Ellmann and Robert O'Clair (New York: W. W. Norton & Co., 1973), 313.
10. James Weldon Johnson, *God's Trombones: Seven Negro Sermons in Verse* (New York: Viking Press, 1955), 14.
11. Julia Cameron, *The Artist's Way: A Spiritual Path to Higher Creativity* (New York: Jeremy P. Tarcher/Putnam, 1992), 18–20.

12. Wilson, *Imagination of the Heart*, 68.
13. Cullen Murphy, *The Word according to Eve* (New York: Houghton Mifflin Co., 1998), 121.
14. Cameron, *Artist's Way*, 79.
15. Kenneth L. Gibble, "Listening to My Life: An Interview with Frederick Buechner," *The Christian Century*, November 16, 1983, 1043.
16. Susan VanZanten-Gallagher, "Mending a Tattered Faith: Devotions with Dickinson" (lecture, Festival of Faith and Writing, Calvin College, Grand Rapids, MI, April 21, 2006).
17. Natalie Goldberg, *Wild Mind: Living the Writer's Life* (New York: Bantam Books, 1990), 10.

Chapter Three: The Plot Thickens

1. Zan Holmes, "Do We Look Like Our Picture?" (Detroit East and West District Leadership Training, Farmington Hills, MI, February 5, 2005).
2. Tim Gautreaux, interview with Darlene Meyering, Festival of Faith and Writing, Calvin College, Grand Rapids, MI, April 22, 2004.
3. John Gardner, *The Art of Fiction: Notes on Craft for Young Writers* (New York: Vintage Books, 1991), 188.
4. Henry Mitchell, "On Preaching to the Whole Person: Part II," *Pulpit Digest*, March/April 1988, 13.
5. Eugene L. Lowry, *The Homiletical Plot: The Sermon as Narrative Art Form* (Westminster John Knox Press, 2001), xx.
6. Ibid., 26.
7. Ibid., 117–21.
8. Ibid., 76.
9. David J. Schlafer, *Surviving the Sermon: A Guide for Those Who Have to Listen* (Boston: Cowley Publications, 1992), 63.
10. Fred Craddock, *Preaching* (Nashville: Abingdon Press, 1985), 177.
11. Henry Mitchell, "On Preaching to the Whole Person: Part I," *Pulpit Digest*, January/February 1988, 54–55.
12. Carlyle F. Stewart III (sermon, Hope United Methodist Church, Southfield, MI, 1994).
13. Tom Russell, "The Sky Above, the Mud Below," *The Rose of the San Joaquin*, CD, High Tone Records, 1995.
14. Craddock, *Preaching*, 176.
15. Sondra Willobee, "Beyond Trembling," (sermon, North Lake United Methodist Church, Chelsea, MI, April 3, 1988).
16. Craddock, *Preaching*, 179.
17. Eugene L. Lowry, *How to Preach a Parable: Designs for Narrative Sermons* (Nashville: Abingdon Press, 1989), 79–114.
18. Ibid., 115–41.
19. Ibid., 142–70.

20. Oprah Winfrey, interview with Michael J. Fox and Tracy Pollan, *O, The Oprah Magazine*, March 2002, 142–49.
21. Charles Wesley, "Come, O Thou Traveler Unknown," *The United Methodist Hymnal* (Nashville: United Methodist Publishing House, 1989), no. 387.
22. Robert C. Tannehill, *The Narrative Unity of Luke-Acts: A Literary Interpretation*, vol. 2, *The Acts of the Apostles* (Minneapolis: Fortress Press, 1990), 7–8.
23. Barbara Brown Taylor, "Blood of the Martyrs," in *Home by Another Way* (Boston: Cowley Press, 1999), 127.
24. Ibid.
25. Ibid., 128.
26. Phyllis Tickle, *What the Heart Already Knows: Stories of Advent, Christmas and Epiphany* (Nashville: Upper Room Press, 1985), 18.
27. John Gardner, *The Art of Fiction: Notes on Craft for Young Writers* (New York: Vintage Books, 1983), 194.
28. Ibid., 192.
29. Answers to "Try This" exercise: (1) Hook: "Jacob is up against it." This hook begins *in medias res.* (2) Complication: Tension within the biblical story is provided by the conflict between Jacob and Esau and by the wrestling match between Jacob and his adversary. The alternation between the biblical story and the contemporary material also escalates the tension and complicates the plot of the sermon. (3) Climax: The detailed story about Michael J. Fox, complete with character, setting, and dialogue, represents the emotional climax of the sermon, culminating with the title phrase, "Limping, but blessed." (4) Resolution: Hymn by Charles Wesley, "Love comes to meet us in the midst of our struggle."
30. Other samples of the collect form can be found in *The Oxford Book of Prayer*, ed. George Appleton (New York: Oxford University Press, 1989), nos. 586, 593, 599, 620, 629, and in Laurence Hull Stookey, *Let the Whole Church Say Amen! A Guide for Those Who Pray in Public* (Nashville: Abingdon Press, 2001), 15–26.

Chapter Four: Finding Stories

1. Tony Campolo, "Spirituality and Social Change" (lecture, Michigan Area School for Pastoral Ministry, Lansing, MI, August 17, 2005).
2. William Hulitt Gloer and Cornelius Plantinga Jr., "Imaginative Reading for Creative Preaching" (lecture, Festival of Faith and Writing, Calvin College, Grand Rapids, MI, April 21, 2006).
3. Ibid.
4. Joel E. Kok, "Permission to Clean the Pasture Spring," continuing education leaflet (Grand Rapids, MI: Calvin Theological Seminary), third panel.
5. Ibid., fourth panel.
6. William D. Cotton, "The Preacher and Contemporary Literature," *Circuit Rider*, May/June 1998, 16.

7. Thomas H. Troeger, *Imagining a Sermon* (Nashville: Abingdon Press, 1990), 61.
8. Abraham Lincoln, Fourth of July Address, July 4, 1858, quoted by Peggy Noonan, *Simply Speaking* (New York: Harper Collins, 1998), 60–61.
9. Charles Denison, *The Artist's Way of Preaching* (Louisville, KY: Westminster John Knox, 2006), 6.
10. Jamie Dean, "Rev. Glenn Wagner Resigns from Calvary Church, Admits Plagiarism," *Charlotte World*, September 13, 2004, http://www.worldnewspaperpublishing.com/news/FullStory.asp?loc=TCW&ID=1251.
11. Anne Lamott, "Forgiveness," in *Traveling Mercies: Some Thoughts on Faith* (New York: Pantheon Books, 1999), 131.
12. Frederick Buechner, *The Sacred Journey* (San Francisco: Harper & Row Publishers, 1982), 2–3.
13. Peter Morgan, *Story Weaving: Using Stories to Transform Your Congregation* (St. Louis: CBP Press, 1986), 102.
14. Sondra Willobee, "The Road Less Travelled" (sermon, First United Methodist Church, Farmington, MI, March 12, 2006), quoting "Welding with Children," by Tim Gautreaux, from his collection of short stories, *Welding with Children* (New York: Picador, 1999), 5–16.
15. Bishop Hope Morgan Ward, "The Calling," audiotape of opening worship, 2006 International United Methodist Clergywomen's Consultation, Chicago, IL, August 13, 2006.
16. Allan Gurganus, *The Oldest Living Confederate Widow Tells All* (New York: Knopf, 1989), 63.
17. John Updike, *In the Beauty of the Lilies* (New York: Random House, 1996), 5.
18. Renni Brown and Dave King, *Self-Editing for Fiction Writers: How to Edit Yourself into Print* (New York: HarperCollins, 1993), 47–55.
19. Sondra Willobee, "Unrolling the Scroll" (sermon, First United Methodist Church, Farmington, MI, January 21, 2007).
20. Walter Wangerin, "My Story, My Self, " Day with Walter Wangerin, sponsored by Psychological Studies and Clergy Consultation Program, Farmington Hills, MI, March 30, 1995.
21. Leander E. Keck, "Limited Resources, Unlimited Possibilities," quoted in Eugene L. Lowry, *How to Preach a Parable* (Nashville: Abingdon Press, 1989), 87.
22. James Denny, quoted in Gordon MacDonald, "Thickburgers and Thin Sermons," http://www.christianitytoday.com/leaders/newsletter/2005/cln50103.html (accessed November 16, 2006).
23. Willobee, "Unrolling the Scroll."
24. Ronald J. Allen, *Preaching: An Essential Guide* (Nashville: Abingdon Press, 2002), 84.
25. Martin Bell, *The Way of the Wolf: The Gospel in New Images* (New York: Seabury Press, 1968), 11–18.

26. Walter Wangerin Jr., *Ragman and Other Cries of Faith* (San Francisco: Harper & Row, 1984), 44–52.
27. Fred Craddock, *The Cherry Log Sermons* (Louisville, KY: Westminster John Knox Press, 2001), 29–30.
28. Debbie Blue, *Sensual Orthodoxy* (St. Paul: Cathedral Hill Press, 2004), 82.
29. Frederick Buechner, *The Sacred Journey* (San Francisco: Harper & Row, 1982), 74.
30. Sondra Willobee, "For All the Saints" (sermon, Whitefield-Grace United Methodist Church, Detroit, November 4, 1984).

Chapter Five: Language of the Incarnation

1. Philip Wheelwright, *The Burning Fountain* (Bloomington: Indiana University Press, 1968), 86–88, quoted in Robert C. Tannehill, *The Sword of His Mouth*, Society of Biblical Literature, Semeia Supplements (Philadelphia: Fortress Press, 1975), 11.
2. Kathleen Norris, "Incarnational Language," *Christian Century*, July 30–August 6, 1997, 699.
3. Janet Burroway, *Imaginative Writing: The Elements of Craft* (New York: Addison, Wesley Longman, 2003), 311.
4. Julia Kasdorf, "'Same! Same!' Pleasures and Purposes of Metaphor" (lecture, Festival of Faith and Writing, Calvin College, Grand Rapids, MI, April 21, 2006).
5. Ibid.
6. Walter Brueggemann, "The Book of Jeremiah: Portrait of the Prophet," *Interpretation: A Journal of Bible and Theology*, vol. 37, no. 2, April 1983, 134–35.
7. Robert C. Tannehill, *The Sword of His Mouth*, Society of Biblical Literature, Semeia Supplements (Philadelphia: Fortress Press, 1975), 11–28.
8. Amos Wilder, *Early Christian Rhetoric* (Cambridge, MA: Harvard University Press, 1971), 84–86.
9. Paul Scott Wilson, *Imagination of the Heart* (Nashville: Abingdon Press, 1988), 144.
10. Fred B. Craddock, *Preaching* (Nashville: Abingdon Press, 1985), 163.
11. Burroway, *Imaginative Writing*, 7.
12. Elizabeth Volpe, "Brewing in Eden," *Rattle: Poetry for the 21st Century*, ed. Tim Green, vol. 26 (Winter 2006): 90.
13. Arthur Miller, *Death of a Salesman*, in *The Portable Arthur Miller*, ed. Harold Clurman (New York: Viking Press, 1971), 33.
14. Interview with Ysaye Barnwell, *The Other Side*, July–August 1997, 47.
15. Reynolds Price, *A Palpable God* (New York: Atheneum Publishers, 1987), 53.
16. Ilya Kaminsky and Katherine Towler, "A Conversation with Franz Wright," *Image: Art, Faith, Mystery*, no. 51 (Fall 2006): 75.
17. Leander Keck, *Paul and His Letters* (Philadelphia: Fortress Press, 1979), 105, 10˜–8.

18. Barbara Brown Taylor, "Lenten Discipline," in *Home by Another Way* (Boston: Cowley Publications, 1999), 65.
19. Barbara Brown Taylor, "Do This and You Will Live" (lecture, Festival of Homiletics, Peachtree United Methodist Church, Atlanta, GA, May 15, 2006); see http://www.barbarabrowntaylor.com/newsletter374064.htm.
20. William Strunk Jr. and E. B. White, *The Elements of Style*, 2nd ed. (New York: Macmillan Publishing Co., 1972), 15.
21. Peggy Noonan, *Simply Speaking: How to Communicate Your Ideas with Style, Substance, and Clarity* (New York: Harper Collins, 1998), 50–51.
22. Norris, "Incarnational Language," 699.
23. Ezra Pound, quoted in William Pratt, *The Imagist Poem: Modern Poetry in Miniature* (New York: E. P. Dutton & Co., 1963), 22.
24. Tim Gautreaux, "Welding with Children," in *Welding with Children* (New York: Picador, 1999), 18–19.
25. Burroway, *Imaginative Writing*, 311.
26. William Hulitt Gloer and Cornelius Plantinga Jr., "Imaginative Reading for Creative Preaching" (lecture, Festival of Faith and Writing, Calvin College, Grand Rapids, MI, April 21, 2006).
27. Craddock, *Preaching*, 164.
28. "Bulwer-Lytton Fiction Contest 2007 Results," Runner-Up, Department of English and Comparative Literature, San Jose State University, San Jose, CA http://www.bulwer-lytton.com/2007.htm.
29. James Earl Massey, *Designing the Sermon* (Nashville: Abingdon Press, 1980), 87.
30. Barbara Brown Taylor, "Way beyond Belief: The Call to Behold," (lecture, Festival of Faith and Writing, Calvin College, Grand Rapids, MI, April 24, 2004). Also available in Jennifer L. Holberg, ed., *Shouts and Whispers: Twenty-one Writers Speak about Their Writing and Their Faith* (Grand Rapids: Eerdmans, 2006).
31. Gabriele Rico, *Writing the Natural Way: Using Right-Brain Techniques to Release Your Expressive Powers* (Los Angeles: J. P. Tarcher, 1983), 17–19.
32. Ibid., 35–36.

Chapter Six: Time to Revise

1. Dorothea Brande, *Becoming a Writer* (New York: Jeremy P. Tarcher/Putnam, 1981), 76–79.
2. Mary Jo Firth-Gillett, Advanced Poetry Workshop, Springfed Arts-Metro Detroit Writers, May 23, 2006.
3. Anne Lamott, *Bird by Bird* (New York: Doubleday, 1994), 18–19.
4. Robert Tuttle, *John Wesley: His Life and Theology* (Grand Rapids: Zondervan Publishing House, 1978), 351.
5. Linda Lee and Wayne Muller, "Come Away with Me: An Experience of Sabbath" (special clergy session, Michigan Area of the United Methodist Church, Lansing, MI, October 28–29, 2002).

6. Ibid.
7. Janet Burroway, *Imaginative Writing: The Elements of Craft* (New York: Addison, Wesley Longman, 2003), 218–19.
8. Eugene L. Lowry, *The Homiletical Plot: The Sermon as Narrative Art Form* (Louisville, KY: Westminster John Knox Press, 2001), 101.
9. Peggy Noonan, *Simply Speaking: How to Communicate Your Ideas with Style, Substance, and Clarity* (New York: Harper Collins, 1998), 34–35.
10. Barbara Brown Taylor, "Way beyond Belief: The Call to Behold" (lecture, Festival of Faith and Writing, Calvin College, Grand Rapids, MI, April 24, 2004). Also available in Jennifer L. Holberg, ed., *Shouts and Whispers: Twenty-one Writers Speak about Their Writing and Their Faith* (Grand Rapids: Eerdmans, 2006).
11. Tim Gautreaux, "Interview with Darlene Meyering" (Festival of Faith and Writing, Calvin College, Grand Rapids, MI, April 22, 2004).
12. Thomas Troeger, "A Sample Visual Sermon for the Mass Media Generation," *Imagining a Sermon* (Nashville: Abingdon Press, 1990), 44–47.
13. Jeffrey Skinner, "Push Hands: Balancing Resistance and Revision," *Poets & Writers*, May/June 2002, 47.
14. Anonymous, "O Sacred Head, Now Wounded," reprinted in *The United Methodist Hymnal* (Nashville: The United Methodist Publishing House, 1989), no. 286.

CPSIA information can be obtained at www.ICGtesting.com
Printed in the USA
BVOW030246211112

305961BV00009B/1/P